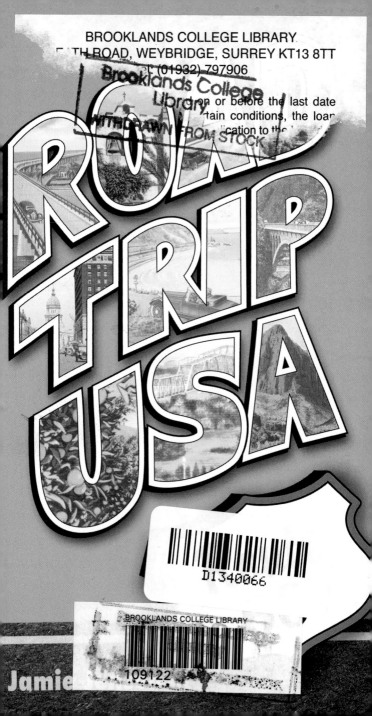

ROAD TRIP USA

Jamie

Contents

ROUTE 66

If you're looking for great displays of neon signs, mom-and-pop motels in the middle of nowhere, or kitschy Americana, do as the song says and "get your kicks on Route 66."

Hollywood	London Bridge	Tinkertown

pg. 104

pg. 92

pg. 57

◄ 420 mi ►   ◄ 400 mi ►   ◄ 250

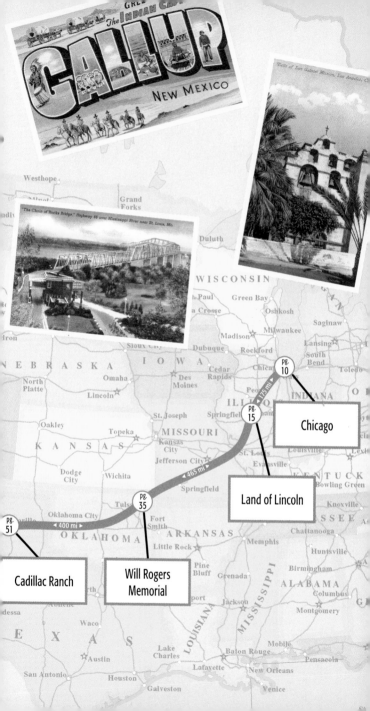

GALLUP NEW MEXICO

"Bells of San Gabriel Mission, Los Angeles, Cal."

"The Chain of Rocks Bridge." Highway 66 over Mississippi River near St. Louis, Mo.

pg. 10

pg. 15

◄ 175 mi ►

Chicago

◄ 465 mi ►

Land of Lincoln

pg. 35

pg. 51

◄ 400 mi ►

Cadillac Ranch

Will Rogers Memorial

Between Chicago, Illinois, and Los Angeles, California

The romance of Route 66 continues to captivate people around the world. Running between Chicago and Los Angeles, "over two thousand miles all the way" in the words of the popular R&B anthem, this legendary old road passes through the heart of the United States on a diagonal trip that takes in some of the country's most archetypal roadside scenes. If you're looking for great displays of neon signs, rusty middle-of-nowhere truck stops, or kitschy Americana, do as the song says and "get your kicks on Route 66."

But perhaps the most compelling reason to follow Route 66 is to experience the road's ingrained time line of contemporary America. Before it was called Route 66, and long before it was even paved in 1926, this corridor was traversed by the National Old Trails Highway, one of the country's first transcontinental highways. For three decades before and after World War II, Route 66 earned the title "Main Street of America" because it wound through small towns across the Midwest and Southwest, lined by hundreds of cafés, motels, gas stations, and tourist attractions. During the Great Depression, hundreds of thousands of farm families, displaced from the Dust Bowl, made their way west along Route 66 to California, following what John Steinbeck called "The Mother Road" in his vivid portrait, *The Grapes of Wrath*. After World War II, many thousands more expressed their upward mobility by leaving the industrial East, bound for good jobs in the suburban idyll of Southern California—again following Route 66, which came to embody the demographic shift from the Rust Belt to the Sun Belt.

Beginning in the late 1950s and continuing gradually over the next 25 years, old Route 66 was bypassed section by section as the high-speed Interstate highways were completed. Finally, in 1984, when the last stretch of freeway was finished, Route 66 was officially decommissioned; the old route is now designated Historic Route 66.

Though it is no longer a main route across the country, Route 66 has retained its mystique in part due to the very same effective hype, hucksterism, and boosterism that animated it through its half-century heyday. It was a Route 66 sight, the marvelous Meramec Caverns, that gave the world the bumper sticker, and it was here on Route 66 that the great American driving vacation first flourished. Billboards and giant statues along the highway still hawk a baffling array of roadside attractions, tempting passing travelers to swim alongside giant blue whales, to see live rattlesnakes and other wild creatures on display in roadside menageries, or to stay at "Tucumcari Tonite."

The same commercial know-how and shameless self-promotion has helped the towns along the old route stay alive. Diners and motels play up their Route 66 connections, and many bona fide Route 66 landmarks are kept in business by nostalgic travelers intent on experiencing a taste of this endlessly endangered American experience. That said, many quirky old motels and cafés hang on by a thread of hope, sit vacant, or survive in memory only—all for want of an Interstate exit. In fact, of all the roads covered in this book, Route 66 has perhaps felt the greatest impact from the modern Interstate world; for many stretches you'll be forced to leave the old two-lane and follow the super slabs that have been built right on top of the old road.

Route 66 passes through a marvelous cross-section of American scenes, from the cornfields of Illinois all the way to the golden sands and sunshine of Los Angeles, passing by such diverse environs as the Grand Canyon, the Native American communities of the desert Southwest, the small-town Midwest heartlands of Oklahoma and the Ozarks, as well as the gritty streets of St. Louis and Chicago. Whether you are motivated by an interest in history, feel a nostalgic yearning for the "good old days" Route 66 has come to represent, or simply want to experience firsthand the amazing diversity of people and landscapes that line its path, Route 66 offers an unforgettable journey into America, then and now.

ILLINOIS

Heading diagonally across the state between Chicago and St. Louis, what remains of Route 66 is a surprisingly rural cruise through endless fields of corn. Despite the urban conglomerations at both ends, for most of its nearly 300-mile trek here,

Route 66 and its modern usurper, I-55, pass along flat prairies with nary a smokestack or skyscraper as far as the eye can see.

The heavy industrial and poverty-stricken hinterlands of Chicago and East St. Louis aren't terribly rewarding for travelers in search of the Mother Road, but a couple of intriguing attractions—one a prehistoric city, the other a water tower shaped like a catsup bottle—are worth searching out. The only real city along Route 66 is the Illinois state capital, Springfield, which has preserved its sections of Route 66 alongside a wealth of places connected to the namesake President here in the "Land of Lincoln." Dozens of small towns across the state play up their Route 66 connections, and most boast at least one true old-road landmark.

Route 66 Across Chicagoland

Following the first (or last) leg of Route 66 across Chicago and its hinterlands is really not worth the effort for anyone except the most die-hard end-to-ender—even Jack Rittenhouse, in his original 1946 *A Guide Book to Highway 66,* didn't bother to describe the route until it reached Plainfield, 35 miles southwest of the Loop. For a symbolic starting point, you can use the grand old Art Institute of Chicago in Grant Park along the lakeshore, since the last US-66 shield used to hang from a streetlight just south of the gallery. If Chicago is your "end of the road," you'll probably prefer to avoid the final few miles of surface streets and make your way to town as quickly as possible via I-55.

At **Plainfield,** a little piece of highway history happened when the original version of Route 66 crossed the even older Lincoln Highway, America's first transcontinental road.

From Lake Michigan, the old road ran west via Adams Street (take Jackson Boulevard eastbound; both are one-way) before angling southwest along Ogden Avenue—a long, diagonal exception to the city's main grid of streets. **Cicero** prides itself on having been a haven to Al Capone and other mobsters during the Prohibition era and now enjoys its Route 66 connections at **Henry's Drive-In,** 6031 W. Ogden Avenue

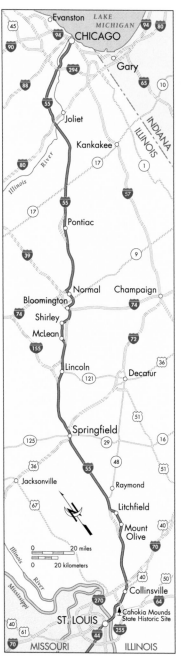

(708/656-9344), where you can snack on excellent Polish hot dogs smothered with a pile of french fries. Neighboring **Berwyn** has lined old Route 66 with a series of glass-block markers but didn't do much to save its most remarkable work of art: **The Spindle,** a tower of ruined cars impaled on a 50-foot steel spike, which stood in the parking lot of a shopping mall until mid-2008, when it was removed in the middle of the night to make way for yet another Walgreen's. (You may have seen The Spindle in the 1990s comedy *Wayne's World.*)

To continue south and west, you have to follow I-55, which was built right on top of old Route 66. In Willowbrook, off Hwy-83 on the north side of I-55 just a dozen miles from the Loop, **Dell Rhea's Chicken Basket** (630/325-0780) at 645 Joliet Road is a welcoming old roadside tavern, with famously fabulous chicken dinners and frequent live music.

Joliet

Joliet, the "City of Steel and Stone," has a rough reputation that doesn't really reflect its welter of historic attractions. Route 66 through this once-mighty

Chicago

New York may have bigger and better museums, shops, and restaurants, and even Los Angeles has more people, but Chicago is still the most all-American city, and one of the most exciting and enjoyable places to visit in the world. Commerce capital of Middle America, where something like 80 percent of the nation's agricultural produce is bought and sold, Chicago's location at the crossroads between the settled East and the wide-open West has helped it to give birth to many new things we now take for granted: the skyscraper, the blues, and the atomic bomb.

Away from The Loop, the skyscraper-spiked lakefront business district that holds the world's tallest and most impressive collection of modern architecture in its oblong square mile, much of Chicago is surprisingly low-rise and residential. Also surprising, considering its inland location, is that Chicago has the highest percentage of immigrants of any American city—300,000 Poles form the largest community outside Warsaw, and Hispanics constitute 20 percent of Chicago's population of three million—with a multi-ethnic character readily apparent in numerous enclaves all over the city. Whatever their origin, however, residents take a particular pride in identifying themselves as Chicagoans, and despite the city's rusting infrastructure, their good-natured enthusiasm for the place can be contagious.

For an unbeatable introduction to Chicago, hop aboard a river cruise offered by the **Chicago Architecture Foundation** (daily May–Nov. only; $30; 312/922-3432). Departing from where the Michigan Avenue Bridge crosses the river and Wacker Drive, these informative and enjoyable tours offer an unusual look up at the city's magnificent towers. Enthusiastic expert guides give the city's general historical background as well as pointed architectural history. North from the river, the "Magnificent Mile" of Michigan Avenue is a bustling shopping strip that holds yet more distinctive towers, along with many of the city's top shops, restaurants, and hotels. Starting

Grant Wood, American. *American Gothic,* 1930. The Art Institute of Chicago: Friends of American Art Collection.

with the gothic-style Tribune Tower—decorated with bits of famous buildings stolen by Tribune staffers from around the globe—and running past the circa-1869 Historic Water Tower at its midpoint, the "Mag Mile" ends in the north with the 95-story John Hancock Center.

Along the lakefront at the heart of downtown, the **Art Institute of Chicago,** 111 S. Michigan Avenue ($12; 312/443-3600), boasts one of the world's great collections of 19th- and 20th-century French painting, and a broad survey of fine art from all over the world. Among its many fine paintings, the Institute also gives pride of place to Grant Wood's *American Gothic,* which he painted as a student and sold to the Institute for $300. North and east of the museum is Chicago's latest great claim to fame: **Millennium Park,** a 25-acre public garden full of fabulous sculptures and a magical, Frank Gehry–designed outdoor concert pavilion that's home to numerous summer concerts and events.

More than just another baseball game, watching the **Chicago Cubs** play at Wrigley Field, 1060 Addison Street (773/404-2827), is a rite of passage that taps into the deepest meanings of the national pastime. Ivy covers the redbrick outfield walls and Chicagoans of all stripes root on the perennial not-quite-winners. The "other" Chicago baseball team, the **White Sox,** play at modern new U.S. Cellular Field (312/674-1000), south of the Loop alongside I-94 at 333 W. 35th Street.

Practicalities

Chicago is home to America's busiest and most infuriating airport, O'Hare (ORD), 17 miles northwest of the Loop and well served by Chicago Transit Authority (CTA) subway trains, shuttle services, and taxis. Chicago's other airport, Midway, is closer to the center of town, and Chicago is also the hub of the national Amtrak system, with trains pulling in to Union Station from all over the country. To get around, you'll really be better off leaving the car behind and riding the CTA elevated train—better known as the "El"—which serves the entire city around the clock.

Chicago has all sorts of top-quality, cutting-edge-cuisine restaurants, but to get a feel for the city you'll be better off stopping at the many older places that have catered to Chicagoans forever. Near the start of old Route 66, **Lou Mitchell's,** 565 W. Jackson Street (312/939-3111), is one of the greatest breakfast and lunch places on the planet. At **Little Al's Italian Beef BBQ,** 1079 W. Taylor Street (312/226-4017), step up to the counter and chow down on a juicy mess of shredded beef soaked with garlicky gravy; this is truly good food. One more classic: **Superdawg Drive-In,** out in the suburbs near O'Hare at 6363 N. Milwaukee Avenue (773/478-7800), where you eat all-beef hot dogs in your car, or soak up the 1940s character in a lively dining room.

Places to stay in Chicago include the moderate likes of the **Best Western River North** ($125 and up; 312/467-0800), at 125 W. Ohio Street, in the trendy River North gallery district, within a quick walk of the "Magnificent Mile" along Michigan Avenue. Chicago's classiest older hotel is the **Drake Hotel** ($200 and up; 312/787-2200), just off the lake at 140 E. Walton Place, with elegant public areas and gracious staff. The most fabulous place to stay may be the **InterContinental** ($200 and up; 312/944-4100), at 505 N. Michigan Avenue, housed in an exuberant space that used to be a Shriner's health club.

The best source of information in advance is the **Chicago Office of Tourism** (877/CHICAGO).

Superdawg Drive-In

industrial enclave is a feast for fans of post-industrial scenery: Loads of old warehouses and commercial buildings line the route, while stalwart bridges cross the historic Illinois & Michigan Canal, which, beginning in the 1840s, connected Chicago with the Mississippi River. Also in Joliet: the now-closed state prison from which John Belushi (a.k.a. "Joliet Jake") is released at the beginning of the 1980 movie *The Blues Brothers.*

South of Joliet, following old Route 66 (Hwy-53) across the I-80 superslab brings you past the massive **Route 66 Raceway** (815/722-5500), where NHRA drag races, NASCAR stock car races, and occasional pop music concerts are held.

Midewin National Tallgrass Prairie Preserve

Along Route 66 between Joliet and Wilmington, a unique undertaking is working to re-create the natural ecosystem on one of the most environmentally damaged areas imaginable: 19,000 acres of the old Joliet Army Ammunition Plant is being converted into the **Midewin National Tallgrass Prairie Preserve** (limited public access; 815/423-6370). Since 1996, when the land was transferred from the Army to the Forest Service, the change from producing TNT to regrowing the native tallgrass prairie has been slow and steady, and after more than 10 years of toxic cleanups and careful husbandry it now offers hiking and biking trails and frequent guided tours of the site. You get a good feeling for the flora and fauna that would have existed naturally in places like this all over the Midwest.

Wilmington and Dwight

From Joliet, you can follow old Route 66 southwest through a series of nice small towns along Hwy-53, which runs along the southeast side of I-55. Though the route is sometimes a bit obscure and not all that rich in history or aesthetic delights, the towns here offer a very pleasant taste of what old Route 66 had to offer: **Dwight** is leafy and quaint with a very fine old Texaco station, **Braidwood** has a set of Burma-Shave signs and the popular, retro-1950s Polka Dot Drive In, while **Wilmington** is semi-famous for the 30-foot-tall Gemini Giant statue that stands outside the **Launching Pad Drive-In** at 810 E. Baltimore Street (815/476-6535).

Pontiac

Some 90 miles southeast of Lake Michigan, the former coal-mining town of **Pontiac** (pop. 11,428) surrounds the stately circa-1875 Livingston County Courthouse. The courthouse's green lawns hold the usual battery of monuments, including one to the namesake Ottawa chief whose visage also graces the General Motors marquee. According to the WPA *Guide to Illinois,* another of these monuments, the Soldiers and Sailors Monument, received the shortest presidential dedication in history when, in 1902, it was "dedicated with a few hasty words by President Theodore Roosevelt, before an audience of less than a dozen people, who congregated briefly under a terrific downpour."

Pontiac is also home to a long-lived Route 66 landmark, the **Old Log Cabin Inn** (815/842-2908) on Pontiac Road on the north edge of town. When the road was rerouted behind the original location, this restaurant was jacked up and flipped around; the old road, which dates from 1918, is still there, behind the café along the railroad tracks.

Bloomington-Normal

Hometown of politician Adlai Stevenson (and Col. Henry Blake of TV's *M*A*S*H*), Bloomington-Normal sits at the middle of Illinois, surrounded by five different Interstate freeways and miles of cornfields. Its main claim to fame is in being the only place in the world where that classic bar snack, **Beer Nuts,** is made; for a free sample (but no tour, alas), stop by the factory (800/BEER-NUT) at 103 N. Robinson Street. The "Twin Cities" are also the corporate home of insurance company State Farm, and birthplace of another all-American icon, the Midwest-based burger chain Steak and Shake, which started here in 1934. Good food is available at characterful **Lucca Grill,** which has been serving pizza and pasta dishes since the 1930s at 116 E. Market Street (309/828-7521).

Funks Grove

Heading on from Bloomington-Normal, westbound drivers will encounter the next two towns in sonorous order—Shirley and McLean—but wordplay aside, the stretch of Illinois farmland between Bloomington and Springfield is rich in Route 66–related heritage. In McLean, 47 miles from Springfield and 15 miles southwest from Bloomington, old Route 66 emerges from the shadow of I-55 and you can follow old Route 66 along the west side of the freeway for just over four miles past the delightful anachronism of **Funks Grove** (309/874-3360), where the friendly Funk family has been tapping trees and making delicious maple sirup (that's how they spell it) since 1891. If you're here in the spring you can watch them tap the trees and hammer in the spouts; each tree can produce four gallons of sap a day, but it takes 50 gallons of sap for each gallon of the final product. Free tastings are available, and a full range of bottles is on sale.

Lincoln

The only town named for Honest Abe in his lifetime, **Lincoln** (pop. 15,418) took his name before he became a famous figure. As a young lawyer, Abraham Lincoln drew up the legal documents for founding the town but warned developers that he "never knew of anything named Lincoln that amounted to much." At the dedication ceremonies, Lincoln supposedly "baptized" the place by spitting out a mouthful of watermelon seeds—hence the plaster watermelon and

historical plaque remembering the great event, next to the train station at Broadway and Chicago Streets in the center of town. Lincoln was also home to Harlem Renaissance poet Langston Hughes (1902–1967), who was elected Class Poet while in the 8th grade here.

Springfield

As the Illinois state capital, **Springfield** (pop. 120,000) embodies the rural small-town character of most of the state and feels much farther away from Chicago than the three-plus-hour drive it actually is, traffic willing. Springfield is also the place that takes the "Land of Lincoln" state's obsession with Abraham Lincoln to its greatest extreme, for it was here that Honest Abe worked and lived from 1837 to 1861. He left Springfield after being elected president and was buried here after his assassination at the end of the Civil War.

There are all manner of Lincoln sights to see all over Springfield, but the newest and best place to start your homage is at the state-run **Lincoln Presidential Museum** (daily; $10; 217/782-5764), across from Union Square Park at 212 N. 6th Street. Once you've toured this comprehensive, reverential yet thought-provoking, $90 million, 200,000-square-foot exhibition, other sights include the only home Lincoln ever owned, his law offices, and of course his tomb. Located in Oak Ridge Cemetery, two miles north of downtown, Lincoln's tomb also includes the remains of his wife and three of four children. Legend has it that if you touch the nose on the bronze bust of Lincoln, good luck will follow.

Though quite sincere and understated, the Lincoln homage can overwhelm, and if you need a change of pace from Lincoln Land there is the beautiful **Dana-Thomas House** (Wed.–Sun.; $5; 217/782-6776) at 301 E. Lawrence Avenue, a half mile south of the state capitol. Designed by Frank Lloyd Wright in 1902, it is the most luxurious, best preserved, and most fully furnished of his houses—and is open for hour-long guided tours. Actually a complete remodel of a

CAPITOL AVENUE, LOOKING WEST, SPRINGFIELD, ILL.

house that already stood on the site, the Dana-Thomas house was built for socialite Susan Dana, who lived here until the late 1920s, when it was sold to a publishing company and used as offices until the state of Illinois purchased it in 1981.

Also worth a look: housed in what some say is the oldest gas station on Route 66, **Shea's Gas Station Museum,** 2075 N. Peoria Road (Wed.–Sat.; 217/522-0475). Curated by the ever-engaging Bill Shea, who has spent the past 50 years right here on Route 66, this petroliana and Route 66 museum displays a photogenic collection of vintage gasoline pumps, signs, shields, and anything else related to sale and use of our favorite fossil fuel.

Springfield also has a favorite Route 66 watering hole, the **Cozy Dog Drive-In** (217/525-1992), on the old road south of downtown at 2935 S. 6th Street. The birthplace of the corn dog, which here goes by the nicer name "Cozy," was founded in 1949 by Ed Waldmire, father of noted Route 66 artist Bob Waldmire. So come on in and chow down—two Cozy Dogs, a drink and a big basket of fries cost around $5.

Almost all the national chain hotels and motels have operations in Springfield, so you shouldn't have trouble finding a room. For a bit of character across from the Lincoln House, and walkably close to everything else in Springfield, consider the **Henry Mischler House,** a Victorian-era B&B at 802 East Edwards Street ($95 and up; 217/525-2660).

Litchfield and Mount Olive

Between Springfield and Cahokia Mounds, the most interesting stretch of old Route 66 runs along the east side of the freeway for over a dozen miles, between Litchfield and Mount Olive. First stop is **Litchfield,** an old coal-mining mining center that is home to one of the best and most stylish Route 66 restaurants, the **Ariston Cafe** (daily;

South of Springfield, on the stretch of old Route 66 that forms the frontage road at I-55 exit 63, near the town of Raymond a marble statue of the Virgin Mary forms a shrine that has become known as **Our Lady of the Highways.**

217/324-2023), right in the heart of town at the junction of old Route 66 and Hwy-16. The food is a step or two up from the usual roadside fare, and the white linen and refined decor have earned it a spot in the Route 66 Hall of Fame. The rest of Litchfield reeks of the old road, with cafés, motor courts, and old billboards aplenty.

Some seven miles southwest of Litchfield, the hamlet of **Mount Olive** (pop. 2,126) was a bustling coal-mining center in the early 20th century. It's now a sleepy little community, where the only signs of its mining past are in the Union Miners Cemetery, along old Route 66 at the northwest edge of town. Near the entrance is a granite shaft rising from an elaborate pedestal, which serves as a memorial to Mary Harris "Mother" Jones (1830?–1930), the celebrated union activist (and liberal-minded magazine namesake) who died here, possibly aged 100, while supporting with a miners' strike. Famous for her passionate oratory, like the phrase "Pray for the dead, and fight like hell for the living," her grave is nearby, marked by a simple headstone.

*Parts of the old road survive **between Springfield and Litchfield,** but the route is incomplete and can be confusing to follow. I-55 makes much shorter work of the 25-mile drive.*

For old-road fans, Mount Olive is also home to the oldest surviving service station on Route 66, the immaculate restored (but no longer in business) Shell station downtown, long owned by Russell Soulsby.

Collinsville: Cahokia Mounds

*Cahokia Mounds sit in the middle of the **American Bottom,** a floodplain whose gunpowder-black alluvial soils have long been considered among the richest and most productive in the world— for example, about 80 percent of the world's horseradish supply comes from right here, making the region the official **Horseradish Capital of the World.** However, Charles Dickens called it an "ill-favored Black Hollow" after enduring its mud, which had "no variety but in depth."*

Old Route 66 followed today's I-270 around the north side of St. Louis, crossing the Mississippi River on the recently restored Chain of Rocks Bridge, but one of southern Illinois's biggest attractions sits directly east of the Gateway Arch, off the I-55/70 freeway at exit 6. Clearly visible to the south side of the Interstate, the enigmatic humps of **Cahokia Mounds State Historic Site** are the remains of the largest prehistoric Indian city north of Mexico. Over 100 earthen mounds of various sizes were built here by the indigenous Mississippian culture while

Europe was in the Dark Ages; the largest covers 14 acres—more ground than the Great Pyramid of Cheops. But don't expect the works of the pharaohs: Symmetrical, grass-covered hills sitting in flat, lightly wooded bottomlands are what you'll find here. The view of the Gateway Arch in distant St. Louis from the 100-foot-top of Monks' Mound lends an odd sense of grandeur to the site, and a sophisticated Interpretive Center (hours vary; 618/346-5160) is a recommended first stop for its exhibits, award-winning multimedia orientation show, and guided and self-guiding tours.

The nearest town to the Cahokia Mounds is **Collinsville,** a pleasant little place that's nearly-world-famous for its 170-foot-high **World's Largest Catsup Bottle,** which rises high above 800 S. Morrison Avenue (Hwy-159), a quarter mile south of Main Street, on the grounds of what used to be the Brooks Catsup Company. This decorated water tower was constructed in 1949 and restored by the people of Collinsville in 1993; it has since been adopted by Collinsville as a super-size symbol of local pride and perseverance.

Not quite on the same scale as the mounds or the catsup bottle, the nearby Route 66 town of Mitchell holds the landmark, 85-year-old **Luna Café,** north of the I-270 freeway along old Route 66 at 201 East Chain of Rocks Road (618/931-3152).

MISSOURI

The Ozark Highlands of southern Missouri, which Route 66 crosses in its 300-odd-mile journey between Illinois and Kansas, are about the only significant hills the road crosses east of Arizona. This plateau region, though not

by any means alpine or breathtaking, is visu-
ally dynamic in a way the broad flatlands of
Illinois or Oklahoma rarely are. Though
the I-44 freeway has replaced the old road
all the way across the state, there are many
signs of older alignments and just about
every Interstate exit drops you within a moment's drive of the Mother Road. Missouri also
holds some great old motels and one of the greatest of the old
Route 66 tourist attractions—Meramec Caverns, an extensive
set of limestone caves offering the most over-the-top underground tour you can take.

Route 66 Across St. Louis

It can be maddening to follow old Route 66 across St.
Louis, but its many great
spots—Ted Drewe's Frozen
Custard Stand, in particular—make it well worth
the effort. One route
crossed the Mississippi
River right into down-
town from Collinsville,
Illinois, while another "City 66" route headed
into downtown St. Louis along Florissant Avenue and
Riverview Drive, after crossing the Mississippi upstream on the
historic **Chain of Rocks Bridge.** The bridge has been renovat-

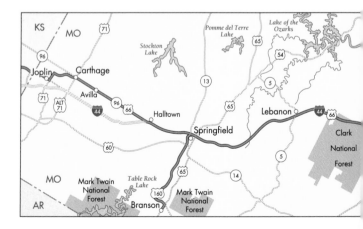

ed for use as a mile-long bike and hiking trail (daylight hours only; 314/741-1211), decorated with an array of old gas pumps and neon signs, just south of the modern I-270 freeway.

Heading southwest out of downtown, the old road followed Gravois Avenue, Chippewa Street, and Watson Road, just south of the parallel I-44 freeway.

Times Beach: Route 66 State Park

There's no plaque or notice proudly marking the spot, but the story of **Times Beach** (pop. 0) deserves mention. Founded in the 1920s as a mountain get-away a dozen miles west of St. Louis along the Meramec River, thanks to Route 66 the town grew into a working-class commuter suburb, with some 2,000 people but no paved streets except for the not-yet-famous highway that passed through the center of town. Times Beach remained a quiet hamlet until 1982, when the federal government discovered that the industrial oil sprayed on streets to keep down dust had in fact been contaminated with toxic dioxin. The toxic waste, combined with a Meramec River flood that buried the town for over a week, made Times Beach uninhabitable.

At Gray Summit, off I-44 at exit 251, a pair of old Route 66 landmarks, the **Diamonds Truck Stop** and the **Gardenway Motel,** still stand along the modern freeway. From here, Hwy-100 runs northwest along the Missouri River to the historic towns of Washington and Hermann.

In 1984 the government paid $33 million to buy Times Beach and tear it down, and 15 years later the cleanup was declared complete. Four hundred acres of what was once Times

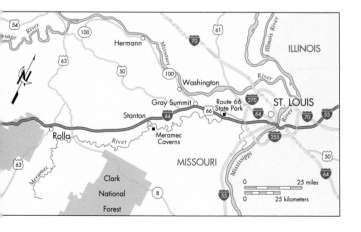

St. Louis

Founded by French fur trappers in 1764, St. Louis served for most of its first century as a prosperous outpost of "civilization" at the frontier of the Wild West. It was the starting point for the explorations of Lewis and Clark, and much later Charles Lindbergh, whose *Spirit of St. Louis* carried him across the Atlantic. Unfortunately, like many other American cities, St. Louis has suffered from years of decline and neglect; the population, which peaked at over 850,000 in 1950, is now less than half that, and the sale of the city's iconic beer, Budweiser, to the Belgian company InBev didn't exactly thrill many locals. Although it has all the cultural and institutional trappings of a major city, not to mention the landmark Gateway Arch, St. Louis is at heart a city of small neighborhoods, such as bluesy Soulard south of downtown, the Italian-American "Hill" (boyhood home of Yogi Berra), and the collegiate West End district near verdant Forest Park.

One thing you have to see when in St. Louis (you literally cannot miss it) is the **Gateway Arch** (daily; 314/655-1700), on the riverfront at the foot of Market Street. Rising up from the west bank of the Mississippi River, Eero Saarinen's stunning 630-foot stainless steel monument still dominates the city skyline, despite the disrespectful rise of nearby office towers. Under the legs of the Arch, which is officially called the Jefferson National Expansion Memorial, the free and fascinating **Museum of Westward Expansion** chronicles the human wave that swept America's frontier west to the Pacific. A small elevator-like tram ($10) carries visitors up the arch to an observation chamber at the very top.

West of downtown around the Washington University campus, in Forest Park's 1,300 beautifully landscaped acres, museums of fine art, history, and science fill buildings that date back to the 1904 World's Fair, St. Louis's world-class swan song.

The **St. Louis Cardinals** (314/421-2400), one of the country's most popular baseball teams, play at retro-modern Busch Stadium, right downtown with views of the river and Gateway Arch.

Practicalities

Freeways and high-speed arteries reminiscent of Los Angeles make a car handy for navigating the St. Louis area—unless you have oodles of money for cab fares—and thanks to the city's sad history of replacing its landmark buildings with blacktop, you'll find plenty of parking lots around downtown.

For food, The Hill neighborhood is hard to beat: **Gian-Tony's** (314/772-4893), at 5356 Daggettt Avenue, is perhaps the best of a dozen classic neighborhood Italian places. Wherever you go, try the toasted ravioli, a local treat. Near Washington University, another great place is the slightly kitschy **Blueberry Hill** (314/727-4444), at 6504 Delmar Boulevard, a retro-1950s diner that has an excellent jukebox, very good burgers, and enough real-life credibility to sometimes attract the likes of St. Louis–born father of rock 'n' roll, Chuck Berry, to play impromptu gigs.

No one leaves St. Louis without cruising old Route 66 southwest from downtown to **Ted Drewe's**, 6726 Chippewa Avenue (314/481-2652), a local institution famous for its many flavors of "concrete"—a delicious frozen dairy-and-egg-custard concoction so thick you can turn it upside down and not spill a drop. Nearby, fried chicken fans flock to **Hodak's**, 2100 Gravois Road (314/776-7292). One last Route 66 place has been going strong for more than 100 years: the **Eat-Rite Diner**, 622 Chouteau Avenue (314/621-9621), a plain blue-and-white cube serving up breakfasts and burgers 24 hours a day (Mon.–Fri.). As the sign says: "Eat Rite, or Don't Eat at All."

St. Louis doesn't have that much of a tourist trade (the muggy weather here in summer keeps most sensible people far away), so places to stay are relatively cheap. **Hampton Inn at Gateway Arch** ($99 and up; 314/621-7900) at 333 Washington Avenue, and the larger **Adam's Mark Hotel** ($125 and up; 314/241-7400) at 112 N. 4th Street, are two of the more popular downtown hotels. Away from the Arch, at the **Marriott at Union Station,** 1820 Market Street ($150 and up; 314/621-5262 or 800/410-9914), the opulently restored lobby, formerly the great rail center's vaulted waiting room, is worth seeing even if you aren't a guest. In another historic reincarnation, a quartet of stately old warehouses has been converted to house the **Westin St. Louis** ($150 and up; 314/621-2000), near the Arch, the river, and the baseball stadium at 811 Spruce Street.

The **St. Louis Convention & Visitors Commission** (314/241-1764 or 800/916-0092) operates a well-stocked information center downtown at 308 Washington Avenue, near the river and I-70.

Adam's Mark Hotel

Beach have since been reopened as the **Route 66 State Park** (daily; free; 636/938-7198) with hiking trails, river access, and a nice little museum on Times Beach and Route 66, housed in a 1930s roadhouse.

Near Times Beach, another Route 66 icon survives along a nice stretch of the old road, between I-44 exits 253 and 264, a mile east of the town of Pacific: the **Red Cedar Inn** served dinner every evening from 1935 to 2005, and now its lovely, warm, woodsy dining room is slated to be used as a local history museum.

Meramec Caverns

The best stop along old Route 66's trek across Missouri, and one of the most enjoyable and charming roadside attractions along the entire Mother Road, **Meramec Caverns** (daily; $20; 573/468-2283 or 800/676-6105) is a set of limestone caves advertised by signs on barns and buildings all along the route, and all over the Midwest. First developed during the Civil War, when the natural saltpeter was mined for use in manufacturing gunpowder, the caves were later popularized as a place for local farmers to get together for dances; the largest room in the caves is still used for Easter Sunrise services and occasional crafts shows and chamber of commerce meetings. An hour west of St. Louis, Meramec Caverns was opened as a tourist attraction in 1935 by Lester Dill, who guided visitors through the elaborate chambers and, more importantly, was a true master of the art of garnering cheap but effective publicity for his tourist attraction. An example: After World War II, Dill sent his son-in-law to the top of Empire State Building dressed up as a caveman and had him threaten to jump off unless everyone in the world visited Meramec Caverns.

Among its many other claims to fame, Meramec Caverns is known as the birthplace of the **bumper sticker.**

Fact and fiction mix freely at Meramac Caverns, adding to the pleasures of seeing the massive caves. Jesse James used these caverns as a hideout, and at least once took advantage of the underground river to escape through the secret "back door." The natural formations are among the most sculptural and delicate of any cave you can visit, and the man-made additions are all low-tech enough to be charming: The hand-operated sound-and-light show ends with a grand finale of Kate Smith singing "God Bless America," while the red, white, and blue of Old Glory is projected onto a limestone curtain.

Detour: Branson

A Middle-American Las Vegas, Branson is a century-old Ozark resort that hit the big time in the 1980s through clever promotion and cunning repackaging of country-and-western music and God-fearing recreation. There are well over 30 major performance venues in Branson, and looking down the list of people who make a living playing here all summer—Jimmy Osmond, Tony Orlando, and Jim "I Don't Like Spiders and Snakes" Stafford—you'd think that anyone who had a hit record or a TV show, or who can sing in a twang and impersonate a country-western star, can have their own showcase theater. Most offer two shows a day plus optional breakfast shows at 10 AM—imagine Hank Williams doing one of those!

Bus tours throng and clog the streets and highways around Branson all summer long, and Branson really does embody just about everything that's annoying and disappointing about the mass-merchandising of "culture"—a cloyingly sentimental version of American

Meramec Caverns is near the town of **Stanton,** 55 miles west of St. Louis, three miles south of I-44 exit 230. There's a small café and a motel on the grounds, which spread along the banks of the Meramec River. At the I-44 exit, the odd little **Jesse James Museum** (daily; $5) insists, despite all evidence to the contrary, that a 100-year-old man who turned up in Stanton in 1948 was in fact Jesse James.

Cuba and Rolla

Along I-44 west of Meramec Caverns, the old Route 66 roadside is lined by ramshackle wooden stands which, toward the end of summer, sell sweet Concord grapes from local Rosati vineyards. The stands are located along the frontage roads (which in many cases are the remnants of the original Route 66), but people park along the freeway and walk to them. At the east edge of this grape-growing district, the small town of **Cuba** has a number of local history murals and the friendly and impossibly inexpensive **Wagon Wheel Motel** ($15 to $25, but worth twice that!; 573/885-3411), at 901 E. Washington Street. Offering 1930s charm music without the slightest sense of humor or moment of sincere feeling. Then again, millions of people like it, so Branson must be doing something right.

What originally put Branson on the tourist map was not music but a book: *The Shepherd of the Hills,* by Harold Bell Wright. Set in and around Branson and published in 1907, it was a huge bestseller. Adapted in the 1930s into an outdoor stage play (417/334-4191), *Shepherd of the Hills* has been drawing millions here ever since.

The Ozark Mountain area around Branson is still a lovely place to explore; just about any road south, east, or west will take you through beautifully scenic mountain landscapes. The single best thing about Branson is **Silver Dollar City** (daily; $29; 417/338-2611), nine miles west of Branson via Hwy-76, a turn-of-the-20th-century theme park devoted to Ozark arts, crafts, and music—and roller coasters. Nearby, you'll find the **Roy Rogers and Dale Evans Museum** (daily; $13; 417/339-1900), at 3950 Green Mountain Drive, where it moved in 2003 from its longtime home in Victorville, California, at the other end of Route 66. Happy Trails!

at 1970s prices, the Wagon Wheel lets you sample a kinder, gentler, less complicated era. (There's also a People's Bank of Cuba, if you're interested in a Fidel-themed photo opportunity.)

Twenty miles on from Cuba, one of the many enduring tourist stops along the Ozark Mountains stretch of Route 66 is the landmark Totem Pole Trading Post (573/364-3519), right off I-44 at the west end of **Rolla** (pop. 16,367; RAW-la). In the center of town, right along old Route 66 on the campus of the Missouri University of Science and Technology (MUST), another draw is the half-scale replica of that ancient Druidical observatory, **Stonehenge.** If you have trouble finding Rolla's Stonehenge, this miniature Wonder of the World stands across Route 66 from the Great Wall of China—a Chinese restaurant. Talk about "small world. . . ."

Waynesville, Lebanon, and the Devil's Elbow

West of Rolla on in to Springfield, I-44 has been built right on top of the old Route 66 corridor, and dozens of old motels, motor courts, gas stations, and other highway-dependent businesses line the remains of the old road, which serves as a frontage road for most of the way. There are plenty of antique shops and cafés to make detours interesting, and the longish detour along old Route 66 through the rugged "Devil's Elbow" district is very memorable, but if you're pressed for time even the Interstate superslab offers a plenty-scenic drive through these upland Ozark Mountains scenes, much of which is protected from development within the Mark Twain National Forest.

Two towns along this stretch grew up along the railroad in the late 1850s, were busy hubs along Route 66, and now boast essential stops for old-roads fans. I-44 traffic, and the 12,000-plus soldiers and dependents at the nearby army base has generated a rash of Wal-Marts and shopping malls in the old Route 66 town of **Waynesville** (pop. 3,500), which stands at the entrance to Fort Leonard Wood U.S. Army base, headquarters of the U.S. Army military police school (and a small museum).

East of Waynesville, old Route 66 followed the undulating Ozarks through the mountains' most rugged stretch, known as the **Devil's Elbow.** The name comes from a section of the Big Piney River that turns so acutely it caused repeated logjams. Until 1981, through here Route 66 followed what's now the very hilly, four-lane **Hwy-Z,** some of the last sections of the old road to be bypassed by I-44.

West of Waynesville, in **Lebanon** (pop. 12,500), the stretch of old Route 66 running along the north side of I-44 holds the marvelous **Munger Moss Motel** ($45; 417/532-3111), at 1336 Route 66, a landmark since 1949, where Ramona Lehman and family offer clean rooms, a wonderful neon sign, and a swimming pool. Across Route 66 from the Munger Moss is a bowling alley with a set of batting cages, making for a perfect Route 66 destination.

Springfield

The largest city in southern Missouri, **Springfield** (pop. 151,580) doesn't feel nearly as big as it is, though it does sprawl for many miles in all directions. Despite the ongoing growth and development Springfield has preserved much of its old Route 66 frontage, along St. Louis Street east of downtown, as well as the grandly named Chestnut Expressway west of downtown. The 20-mph speed limit on downtown streets—and tons of free parking—enables Route 66 pilgrims to pay homage to the town's Arabesque landmark **Shrine Mosque** theater, at 601 E. 1st Street, which it still hosts occasional concerts.

Springfield is home to the Class AA Texas League **Springfield Cardinals**, who play off US-65 at one of the country's most attractive ballparks, Hammons Field (417/863-2143).

Springfield is also celebrated as the place where "Wild" Bill Hickok killed fellow gambler Dave Tutt, apparently because Tutt wore the watch he'd won from Hickok playing cards. A plaque in the central square tells one of many variations on the tale.

One place you have to see to believe—though the fisherman or hunter in your family will already know about it, for sure—is "The World's Greatest Sporting Goods Store," **BASS Pro Shops Outdoor World** (417/887-7334), at 1935 S. Campbell Street. Along with acres of floor space, this Granddaddy of all sporting goods stores, birthplace of what is now an international chain, has a 140,000-gallon fish tank, a 40-foot waterfall, and even its own McDonald's.

Springfield has at least one fine old Route 66 motel: the **Route 66 Rail Haven** ($75 and up; 417/866-1963), at 203 S. Glenstone Avenue on the corner of old Route 66 and US-65. Open since 1938, it has been fully modernized and now is a Best Western affiliate with a railroad theme. A mile away on old Route 66 is one of the earliest and most stylish models of the **Steak and Shake** burger chain (417/866-6109); located at 1158 E. St. Louis Street and open 24 hours, this is one of the last ones where carhops still bring you your food (during daylight hours).

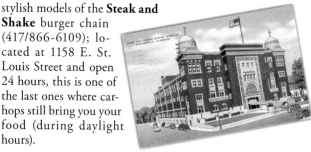

Carthage

Just shy of the Kansas border, six miles north of I-44 and right on old Route 66, **Carthage** (pop. 12,688) is a perfect little

A great stretch of old Route 66, renumbered Hwy-96, runs for 50 miles along the north side of I-44 between Springfield and Carthage, passing rolling pastures and little towns like **Halltown** and **Avilla,** with antique shops and abandoned cafés lining the old highway frontage.

Carthage was the boyhood home of naturalist **Marlin Perkins,** host of *Mutual of Omaha's Wild Kingdom* TV show. A life-sized statue of him stands in Central Park, three blocks southwest of the courthouse square. Carthage was also the girlhood home of Wild West outlaw **Belle Starr.**

town, looking for all the world like the model for the idyllic though fictional town of Hill Valley from the *Back to the Future* movies. The center of Carthage is dominated by the outrageously ornate, circa-1895, limestone Jasper County Courthouse, which features a local history mural and an open-cage elevator in the lobby. The rest of the town is fairly franchise-free—away from the Interstate at least—and the residential areas hold well-maintained Victorian houses.

For fun on the road, there's a bowling alley, **Star Lanes** (417/358-2144), at 219 E. 3rd Street, just east of the square. A mile or so west of downtown on Old Route 66, enjoy a double feature of Hollywood blockbusters in the comfort of your car at the **66 Drive-In** (weekends only; 417/359-5959), at 17231 Old 66 Boulevard.

If you have a soft spot for hyperbolic sentimentality, one not-to-be-missed monument is the **Precious Moments Chapel** (daily; free; 417/358-7599), featuring the wide-eyed characters from the religious figurine series. The chapel is well signed, west of US-71 on the southwest edge of Carthage.

The 1940s stainless steel landmark **Iggy's Diner** (daily; 417/237-0212) is not far away, at 2400 Grand Avenue, while downtown Carthage has another good place to eat, the **Carthage Deli,** 301 S. Main Street (417/358-8820), which serves sandwiches and milk shakes in a 1950s-style soda fountain on the northwest corner of the courthouse square. Within a short walk is an elegant B&B, the **Leggett House** ($100; 417/358-0683), at 1106 Grand Avenue.

Also in Carthage is an old Route 66 landmark: the glowing red-and-green neon sign of the **Boots Motel,** 107 S. Garrison Street. Clark Gable stayed here, and it remained a welcoming, family-run place until the late 1990s. Boots has been closed for years and was for sale at time of writing.

Joplin

If you want to travel the old Route 66 alignment across

Kansas, you'll also pass through **Joplin** (pop. 45,504), a border town that's the industrial center of the tri-state region. Formerly a lead- and zinc-mining town, Joplin is not an especially photogenic place, better known for its high-quality limestone than for its history, though highway heritage is well served at Schifferdecker Park, west of downtown off 7th Street, a pre–Route 66 rest area that now has a mining museum, small Route 66 museum, and a public swimming pool that is much appreciated on a sweltering late summer day. Though many of its businesses have fled to the fringes, Joplin's downtown area does hold one unlikely attraction, a vibrant mural by artist Thomas Hart Benton depicting life in Joplin at the turn of the 20th century. The mural, which turned out to be the artist's final complete work, is in the lobby of the Joplin City Hall, east of Main Street at 303 E. 3rd Street.

Southeast of Joplin, near the town of Diamond, the **George Washington Carver National Monument** (417/325-4151) preserves the farm where the eminent agricultural scientist, educator, and self-suffiency advocate grew up in the 1860s.

On the Kansas/Missouri border, tune to **KRPS 89.9 FM** for classical music and NPR news.

KANSAS

The shortest but perhaps best-signed stretch of Route 66's eight-state run is its 13.2-mile slice across the southeast corner of Kansas. Be careful not to blink your eyes, or you'll be saying, as Dorothy did in *The Wizard of Oz,* "I think we're not in Kansas anymore."

Coming from Missouri, your first town in Kansas is **Galena,** where the funky **Galena Mining and Historical Museum** (hours vary; 620/783-2192), just off the main drag and marked by a big "Old 66" sign at 319 W. 7th Street, is stuffed with old newspaper clippings and other items that give a glimpse of town life during its 1920s-era mining heyday. At its peak, Galena had a population near 30,000 (10 times the current number), and various rusting tools and machines testify to the work that once went on here. That said,

One of the Lead and Zinc Mines in the Tri-State Mining District of Missouri-Kansas-Oklahoma

Massive lead mines like this have disappeared from Kansas.

the hospitable Route 66 spirit lives on inside the old "Kan-O-Tex" gas station, now serving fast-food and souvenirs, especially those related to Pixar's animated Route 66 movie *Cars*. (The old tow truck that apparently inspired the character Tow Mater is parked outside, though they've had to change its name to avoid the wrath of Disney's lawyers.)

Another appetizing attraction awaits in **Riverton,** the next town along, where the **Old Riverton Store** (620/848-3330), a.k.a. "Eisler Brothers," has been open since the 1920s. Across the highway from a big power plant, the old store is now headquarters of the small but active Kansas Route 66 Association and an essential stop for fans of the old road.

Heading west towards Oklahoma, the newer highway bypasses a fine old rainbow-arched Route 66 concrete bridge, just east of **Baxter Springs,** where locals point with pride at the old bank (once robbed by Jesse James, and now a café and B&B!) and the nicely restored, 1930s Phillips 66 filling station, now a useful museum and **information center** (620/856-2066) at 10th Street and Military Avenue (a.k.a. Route 66).

Though it's pretty quiet these days, during the Civil War Baxter Springs saw one of the worst massacres in the country's history, when nearly 100 Union soldiers, including many African Americans, were captured and killed by William Quantrill's rebel Confederate raiders (including the aforementioned Jesse James), who had disguised themselves by wearing blue Union uniforms. A monument to the soldiers stands in **Baxter Springs National Cemetery,** the second-oldest military cemetery in the nation, off US-166 two miles west of town.

OKLAHOMA

Apart from occasional college football teams, Oklahoma doesn't often get to crow about being the best in the country, but as far as Route 66 is concerned, the state is definitely num-

ber one. Containing more still-drivable miles of the old highway than any other state, Oklahoma is definitely mecca for old-roads fans.

Underneath the promotional hoopla that Route 66 generates everywhere it ever went, all over the state you can see signs that barely a century ago all of Oklahoma was Indian Territory, last refuge of Kiowa, Apache, Comanche, and other tribes before the U.S. government took even this land away from them during "land rushes" in the 1890s. A few years later, oil was discovered and the state started on one of a series of boom-and-bust cycles. The Dust Bowl exodus of the 1930s was the greatest downturn, as thousands of Oklahoman families headed west on Route 66, though many of the towns along the road take bittersweet pride in *The Grapes of Wrath* connections.

Oklahoma has the longest and most intact stretches of old Route 66, and if you really want to explore it to the fullest, get your hands on a copy of the essential map-packed road guide *Oklahoma Route 66,* by Arcadia, Oklahoma's own Jim Ross.

Northeast Oklahoma: The Sidewalk Highway

In the far northeastern corner of Oklahoma, old Route 66 runs through a hardscrabble former lead- and zinc-mining region, from the Kansas border to Vinita on the I-44 Turnpike. Three miles southwest of the Kansas border, **Quapaw** could be the first or last Oklahoma town you visit, depending upon your direction, but either way it's worth a look for the many murals painted on the walls of downtown businesses. The next town along, **Commerce** (pop. 2,426), was another old mining town, noteworthy as the boyhood home of the late, great Yankee player Mickey Mantle, in whose honor the old Route 66 alignment down Main Street has been renamed. Four miles to the south via old Route 66 (now signed as US-69), **Miami** holds the magnificent Spanish Revival–style Coleman Theater, built in 1929 when the town was still luxuriating in the riches coming out of the surrounding mines.

Still following US-69, now roughly parallel to (and eventually under) I-44 between Miami and Afton, some of the earliest paved stretches of old Route 66 were constructed only one lane wide, because in 1926 the state of Oklahoma did not have enough money to build a full-width version. Not surprisingly, these lengths of the road became known as the **"Sidewalk Highway."** The easiest stretch to find runs parallel to US-69—turn west at the Northeast Technology Center vocational school along an increasingly narrow country lane, and look out for the "66" shields painted on the pavement. This "Sidewalk Highway" rejoins the main Route 66 alignment at Afton, near the fabled but faded Buffalo Ranch Trading Post.

Vinita

Old Route 66 crosses the Interstate (a.k.a. the Will Rogers Turnpike) again at **Vinita,** where the region's Native American heritage is brought into focus at the **Eastern Trails Museum** (Wed.–Fri. 1–4 PM; free; 918/256-2115), next to the public library at 215 W. Illinois Street. The exhibits center on the Cherokee Trail of Tears, which brought the tribe here after a forced march from North Carolina in the 1830s, but the museum also covers the general history of the surrounding area.

Vinita is home to the **Will Rogers Memorial Rodeo,** held here each August since 1935, the year he died; Rogers attended secondary school in Vinita after growing up near Claremore. Vinita also hosts the annual **World's Largest Calf Fry Festival** in mid-September. (Calf fries are prairie oysters, otherwise known as beef testicles. Just so you know.) Contact the **visitors center** (918/256-7133) for details on any of these.

Vinita also has a great old Route 66 restaurant: **Clanton's Cafe** (918/256-9053), right at the center of town at 319 E. Illinois Street. "Oklahoma's oldest family-owned and operated restaurant," since 1927 Clanton's has been famous for its chicken-fried beefsteak, served here with mashed potatoes and slathered in peppery white gravy. Clanton's also has good burgers and, in case you miss the festival, calf fries. (See above for a disclaimer.)

Foyil

Between Vinita and Claremore, old Route 66 survives in regular use as the "Free Road" alternative to the I-44

Turnpike, alternating between two-lane and divided four-lane highway. The most interesting wide spot along this stretch of hallowed road is **Foyil,** where in the 1940s and 1950s retired fiddle-maker and folk artist Ed Galloway sculpted an outdoor garden of giant totem poles—the tallest is over 90 feet—and other Native American–inspired objects out of concrete. After fading and weathering for many years, the poles, four miles east of town via Hwy-28A, were restored in 1993–1994 as **Totem Pole Park** (daily dawn–dusk; free), and now it's a fascinating place to stop for a picnic or to simply admire the effort that went into these "Watts Towers of the Plains."

Foyil was the hometown of Andy Payne, the Cherokee youth who in 1928 won the **"Bunion Derby,"** a coast-to-coast foot race that followed Route 66 from Los Angeles to Chicago, then headed east to New York City—equivalent to running a marathon and a half every day for the 86 days it took him to finish.

Claremore: Will Rogers Memorial

Twenty miles northeast of Tulsa, **Claremore** (pop. 15,873) is a bigger-than-average Route 66 town, one that will be forever connected with its favorite son, Will Rogers. Rogers was born nearby in a rough log cabin "halfway between Claremore and Oologah before there was a town at either place," on November 4, 1879. He rose from a vaudeville career as a side-show rope-tricks artist to become one of the most popular figures in America, thanks to his folksy humor.

Will Rogers starred on Broadway for 10 years in the *Ziegfield Follies,* wrote an immensely popular newspaper column, and acted in over 70 Hollywood movies. Sadly, before he could retire back home to Claremore, Rogers was killed in a plane crash in 1935; his land was later turned into the **Will Rogers Memorial** (daily; donations; 918/341-0719), a mile west of downtown Claremore on a hill overlooking the town.

A statue of Rogers greets visitors at the front door, and his tomb is here, along with a small archive and museum that recounts his life story, showing off his collections of saddles, lariats, and other cowboy gear.

Will Rogers

Another popular Claremore stop is the **J. M. Davis Arms and Historical Museum** (closed Sun.; donations; 918/341-5707), right off Route 66 at 333 N. Lynn Riggs Boulevard.

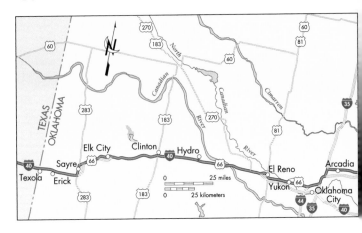

Besides one of the largest and most comprehensive gun collections anywhere in the world (over 20,000 firearms!), the museum has antique musical instruments, hundreds of posters dating back to World War I, and 1,200 German beer steins.

For good food and out-of-this-world pies (over a dozen different kinds), stop by the **Hammett House,** west of downtown next to the Rogers Memorial, 1616 W. Will Rogers (918/341-7333).

Catoosa: The Blue Whale

One of Tulsa's premier Route 66 attractions was the giant **Blue Whale,** in the suburb of **Catoosa**, northeast of Tulsa along the stretch of the old road that runs from I-44 exit 240. The park, built as an animal-themed tourist attraction in the 1970s by Hugh Davis, a curator at the Tulsa Zoo, closed down long ago and was left to crumble. Unlike so many other long-suffering Route 66 landmarks, however, the Blue Whale has been lovingly restored by the family of its original creators (with a little help from the Hampton Inn brand of Hilton Hotels).

Catoosa, surprisingly, is also a major port, linked, by way of impressively engineered improvements to the Arkansas River system, to the Gulf of Mexico.

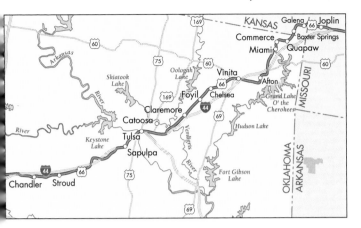

Tulsa

Home to fine art deco buildings built during the 1920s boom years of the Oklahoma oil industry, and the Gilcrease Museum, one of the country's top art museums, **Tulsa** (pop. 385,000) is a bustling big city that doesn't make a song-and-dance out of its many treasures. It's a fascinating place to explore, but if your time is limited, spend it at the **Gilcrease Museum** (daily; 918/596-2700), on the northwest edge of Tulsa. Bought with the fortune benefactor Thomas Gilcrease made when oil was discovered on his land, the collection includes some of the most important works of Western American art and sculpture, with major works by Thomas Moran, George Catlin, and others, plus Native

Tulsa is the home of **Oral Roberts University,** marked by a futuristic, 15-story tower and an 80-foot-high pair of praying hands along Lewis Avenue, six miles south of downtown.

American artifacts and early maps that put the frontier region into its historical contexts. The expansive grounds include a lovely series of gardens and Mr. Gilcrease's old house, now home to the Tulsa Historical Society, which displays photographs and objects related to the evolution of the city and the state.

For dinner or a drink, the liveliest part of Tulsa is the

Books on Route 66

Considering the old road's great fame, it's hardly surprising that over a dozen different books in print deal with the Route 66 experience. Some are travel guides, some folk histories, others nostalgic rambles down what was and what's left along the Mother Road. Photographic essays document the rapidly disappearing architecture and signage, and at least one cookbook catalogs recipes of dishes served in cafés on the route. The following is a sampling of favorite titles, most of which can be found in stores along the route if not in your local bookstore.

- *The Grapes of Wrath,* John Steinbeck (Viking, 1937). The first and foremost Route 66–related story, this compelling tale traces the traumatic travels of the Joad family from Dust Bowl Oklahoma to the illusive Promised Land of California. Brutally vivid, *The Grapes of Wrath* was an instant bestseller at the tail end of the Depression and was the source of Route 66's appellation, "The Mother Road."

- *A Guide Book to Highway 66,* Jack Rittenhouse (University of New Mexico, 1989). A facsimile reprinting of the self-published 1946 book that the late author

Brookside district, south of downtown around 34th Street and Peoria Avenue, where there's a handful of trendy cafés, nightclubs, and restaurants. There's hardly anything left along old Route 66, but you can get a feel for the old days downtown at the retro 1920s **New Atlas Grill,** 415 S. Boston Street (918/583-3111), serving full breakfasts plus soups, salads, and lunchtime sandwiches in an art deco tower. If you want a taste of the 1950s, you'll probably enjoy the good honest food at **Tally's Good Food Café,** a retro-Route 66 diner just off Midtown Tulsa's 11th Street alignment, east of the University of Tulsa campus at 1102 S. Yale Avenue (918/835-8039).

sold door-to-door at truck stops, motor courts, and cafés along the route.

- *Route 66: The Illustrated Guidebook to the Mother Road,* Bob Moore and Patrick Grauwels (RoadBook International, 2002). The most-detailed driver's guide to old Route 66, packed with mile-by-mile instructions and information as well as photographs and illustrations, spiral-bound for on-the-road ease of use.

- *Route 66: The Mother Road,* Michael Wallis (St. Martin's Press, 1987). This richly illustrated and thoroughly researched guide to the old road is more armchair companion than practical aid, but the book captures the spirit of Route 66, and the writer has been a key promotional force behind the road's preservation and rediscovery.

- *Route 66 Traveler's Guide,* Tom Snyder (St. Martin's Press, 1990). A state-by-state description of Route 66, with an emphasis on the stories behind the sights you see. Illustrated with 1930s-era auto club maps adapted to show the path of modern freeways but still evoking the spirit of the old road.

- *Searching for 66,* Tom Teague (Samizdat House, 1996). More personal than other titles on Route 66, this book of vignettes describes the author's interactions with the many people along Route 66 who have made it what it is. As a bonus, the book is illustrated with the fine pen-and-ink drawings of Route 66 artist Bob Waldmire.

The usual chain hotels and motels line all the freeways, and there's a big **Ramada Inn** ($75 and up; 918/585-5898) downtown at 17 W. 7th Street. For the full Route 66 experience, try the saguaro-signed **Desert Hills Motel,** just east of Tally's at 5220 E. 11th Street ($60 and up; 918/834-3311).

Old Route 66: Sapulpa and Stroud

West from Tulsa, old Route 66 snakes back and forth beside I-44 for a dozen miles of eye-blink small towns and abandoned motor courts (most of them built of local rocks). Near the east end of this stretch, three miles west of bustling

Sapulpa, the circa-1921 **Rock Creek Bridge** is a reminder of what the old roads were really like: 120 feet long yet only 12 feet wide, the truss is rusty but the bridge still stands as a proud reminder of the original 1920s Route 66. Across the bridge is another evocative reminder: a drive-in movie theater, now closed but with the screen and the fan-shaped parking lot still intact.

West of Sapulpa, old Route 66 zig-zags back and forth along the freeway for the next 25 miles. One stop to keep in mind, **Russ's Ribs** (918/367-5656), at 233 S. Main Street in the brick-paved heart of **Bristow,** is home to some of the best $3 barbecue sandwiches on the planet. A full slab will set you back around $15, and Russ also makes some excellent deli sandwiches and "family packs" with all the fixin's for a road-side picnic.

Continuing west, old-roads fanatics will probably want to follow the winding alignment of Route 66, which continues along the south side of the turnpike for over 40 miles. On the west side of **Stroud** (pop. 2,758; "Home of Daneka Allen, Miss OK 1999"), check out the **Rock Cafe** (918/968-3990), at 114 W. Main Street, a Route 66 relic built in 1939 out of paving stones from the original highway and still churning out its better-than-average roadside fare. The Rock Café (whose bathroom featured original graffiti by *Toy Story* creator John Lasseter, who modeled some scenes in his Route 66 movie *Cars* on the Rock Café's inimitable architecture) suffered from a fire in 2008 but promises to be back up and running by the time you get there. Stroud also has the classic old **Skyliner Motel,** at 717 W. Main Street ($50 and up; 918/968-9556).

Chandler and Arcadia

West of Stroud, as for most of the way between Tulsa and Oklahoma City, old Route 66 continues along the south side of the I-44 Turnpike, which has another of its very rare exits at

Chandler. **Chandler** (pop. 2,842) is one of the most pleasant old Route 66 towns in Oklahoma and stands out from its top-notch colleagues for a number of good reasons, not least of which is

the classic **Lincoln Motel** ($45; 405/258-0200), at 740 E. 1st Street, along old Route 66 at the east edge of town. It's still as neat and tidy as the day it opened in 1939—two dozen two-room cabins, each with an American flag and a pair of yellow lawn chairs for watching the world whiz by.

Heading west toward Oklahoma City, old Route 66 continues along the south side of I-44, crossing under the freeway about four miles west of Chandler, where there's a metal-roofed barn emblazoned with a photogenic "Meramec Caverns—Stanton MO" sign. From here, one of the state's best surviving stretches of Route 66, known locally as the "Free Road," runs for over 30 miles along the north side of the turnpike, passing by horse and cattle ranches as it rolls across the red earth. About 10 miles east of the I-35 freeway through OKC, the main stop along this idyllic rural cruise is the old highway town of **Arcadia** (pop. 320), which holds a wonderfully restored, very large red **round barn.** The ground floor of this much-loved landmark, originally built way back in 1898, is now a mini museum and gift shop (405/396-2761) selling some highly collectible original Route 66 memorabilia.

A half mile east of the round barn, Arcadia's other Route 66 landmark is bright, shiny, and new: **Pops,** a gas station and small café fronted by a giant (66-foot-tall) soda pop bottle–shaped sign (not neon, but multicolored energy-efficient LEDs). Built by Aubrey McClendon, the Oklahoma-born coal-mining millionaire who funded the "Swift Boat" attacks against John Kerry

North of OKC, Route 66 ran through the town of **Edmond,** the place where aviator **Wiley Post** is buried (he was the pilot killed in the same crash as **Will Rogers**). Edmond is also notorious for the fact that a disgruntled post office employee killed 14 of his co-workers here in 1986, inspiring the expression **"going postal."**

Following old Route 66 across Oklahoma City can be confusing, but keep an eye peeled for the **Route 66 Bowl** on 39th Street; a **bottle-shaped building** on Classen Boulevard at 23rd Street NW, across from a 50-year-old gold-leaf geodesic dome; and a **retro McDonald's** featuring a "Speedie" sign and carhop service, on the nearby corner of 23rd Street and Pennsylvania Avenue.

OIL GUSHER AT OKLAHOMA CITY, OKLA.—76

in 2004, Pops opened in 2007 and sells over 400 different varieties of soda pop, as well as the requisite burgers and fuel.

Oklahoma City

Now tragically synonymous with the terrorist bombing carried out by Timothy McVeigh in 1995, **Oklahoma City** (pop. 506,132) has long been one of the primary stops along the Mother Road. In the Bobby Troup song, it was the only place along the route he singled out for praise, no doubt more for the easy rhyme ("Oklahoma City is mighty pretty") than for its less obvious visual charms. The city was the biggest boomtown of the 1889 Land Rush, when Oklahoma was opened for white settlement after being set aside "for eternity" as Indian Territory. Between noon and sundown on April 22, over 10,000 people raced here to claim the new lands—many of them having illegally camped out beforehand, earning the nickname "Sooner," which is still applied to the state's college football team.

A second boom took place during the Depression years, when oil was struck; there are still producing wells in the center of the city, including some on the grounds of the state capitol. The collapse of the oil industry in the 1980s hit hard, but the shock of the 1995 bombing seems to have galvanized the city, which has since revitalized itself with a gorgeous new baseball stadium, a concert arena, and canal-side cafés in the Bricktown warehouse district south of downtown.

Right on old Route 66 across from the capitol, a good first stop is the **Oklahoma Museum of History** (closed Sun.; free; 405/521-2491), at 2100 Lincoln Boulevard, which has exhibits tracing the state's history, with special collections on the Native American presence, on pioneers, and on the oil industry. There's also a wide-ranging oral history of the Mother Road.

The Class AAA **Oklahoma Redhawks** (405/218-1000) play at ever-pleasant Bricktown Ballpark, south of downtown near the junction of I-35 and I-40. Games are broadcast on **WKY 930 AM.**

OKC now has an NBA team, the **Oklahoma City Thunder** (405/208-4600), formerly known as the Seattle SuperSonics.

It can be hard to go about your nostalgic Route 66 tour in the aftermath of the April 19, 1995, bombing of the Alfred P. Murrah Federal Building, where 168 men, women, and children were killed. Between the capitol and Bricktown, the site of the bombing has been preserved as a **memorial park** (open 24 hours; free), landscaped with a shallow pool around which are arrayed a series of 168 sculpted chairs. Each chair represents a person killed in the blast, and the chairs range from very small to full-sized, marking the varying ages of the dead (who included 19 kids from the building's day-care center.) An adjacent **museum** (daily; $7; 405/235-3313) tells the story of the bombing, its perpetrators, and its victims.

Oklahoma City Practicalities

Downtown OKC spreads northwest from the busy I-35/I-40 junction ("The Crossroads of America"), where a massive new **American Indian Cultural Center** (405/239-5500) is under development. On the west side of the freeway, the Bricktown district is home to many fun restaurants and bars like **Tapwerks Ale House** (405/319-9599), at 121 E. Sheridan Avenue, which has great beers, good food, and frequent live music. Oklahoma City also has more barbecue stands and steakhouses than just about anywhere in the country: One old Route 66 landmark, the Kentucky

Club speakeasy and roadhouse once frequented by Pretty Boy Floyd, still survives as the **Oklahoma County Line** (405/478-4955), an upscale barbecue restaurant on the northeast edge of town, near the National Cowboy Hall of Fame at 1226 NE 63rd Street. For great food right on old Route 66, go to the popular **Ann's Chicken Fry House** (405/943-8915), near Jack's BBQ at 4106 NW 39th Street—look for the classic Caddies and fake police cars in the parking lot. Or if you're feeling adventurous, step inside that bottle-shaped building at 2426 NW Classen, where **Banh Mi Ba Le** (405/478-2250) serves delicious Vietnamese food (OKC is home to more than 10,000 Vietnamese-Americans).

Accommodation options in and around OKC are provided by the usual motel chains, plus the **Hospitality Inn** ($60 and up; 405/942-7730), on Route 66 at 3709 N.W. 39th Street.

El Reno

Established as Fort El Reno in 1874 as part of U.S. Army efforts to subdue the Cheyenne, **El Reno** (pop. 16,212) later saw duty as a POW camp during World War II. More recently, the

For westbound travelers, El Reno marks the first appearance of one of the **longest-running ad campaigns** along Route 66: dozens of billboards advertising "Tucumcari Tonite," 350 miles from its New Mexican subject.

West of Oklahoma City, old Route 66 runs along the north side of I-40; in places it's a three-lane road, with a dangerous passing lane in the center. The first real town beyond the OKC suburbs is **Yukon,** hometown of country crooner **Garth Brooks** and of a giant "Yukon's Best Flour" grain mill, whose huge sign lights up the night sky and draws shutterbugs off the highway.

town earned a measure of fame as the site of a motel seen in the offbeat road movie *Rain Man.* (In the movie, the motel was in Amarillo, but the "real" one, called the Big Eight, sat along old Route 66 at the east edge of El Reno.)

For hungry road-trippers, especially those fond of all-American burger joints, El Reno offers an abundance of choices. Three great old places stand within a block of old Route 66, which followed Wade Street across downtown. The oldest, **Robert's** at 300 S. Bickford Street (405/262-1262), has been cooking since 1926. A block to the west is **Sid's Diner,** at 300 S. Choctaw Street (405/262-7757), while a block to the east is **Johnnie's Grill** (daily; 405/262-4721), at 301 S. Rock Island, famed for its Fried Onion Burgers. (On the first weekend in May, El Reno gets together to cook up the "World's Largest Hamburger," a 750-pound behemoth that inspires an all-day festival.)

Hydro: Lucille's

There's no clearer contrast between the charms of the old road and the anonymity of the Interstate than tiny **Hydro,** midway between Oklahoma City and Clinton on the west bank of the Canadian River. A wonderful length of old Route 66 runs along the north side of I-40 exit 89, right past the ancient service station and souvenir stand operated by Lucille Hammons from 1941 until her death, at age 85, in August 2000. Though it's just 50 yards from the fast lane of the freeway, visiting Lucille's place to buy a soda or a postcard and have a quick hello with the energetic proprietor was a Route 66 rite of passage.

West of Lucille's, a surviving six-mile stretch of old Route 66 pavement follows the lay of the land up and down, offering a better sense of the landscape than does the faster but duller new road, which was completed in 1966.

Clinton

Named for Judge Clinton Irwin and not for former President Bill, **Clinton** (pop. 8,833) started life as a trading post for local

Cheyenne Arapahoe people and is now in the spotlight as home of the official **Oklahoma Route 66 Museum** (daily, closed Sun. and Mon. in winter; $3; 580/323-7866), near the west end of town at 2229 W. Gary Boulevard. Unlike many other "museums" along the route, this one is a true showcase and not just another souvenir stand. Funded by a variety of state and local sources, the museum reopened in late 1995 after undergoing a massive, million-dollar expansion and improvement and is one of the better museums of the old road along the old road. Collectors from all over the country, including Clinton's own Gladys Cuthbert, whose husband, Jack Cuthbert, was the primary promoter of Route 66 throughout its glory years, donated signs, artifacts, and memorabilia which have been organized into a comprehensive exhibition of Mother Road history and culture not to be missed by any Route 66 aficionado. (There's a good gift shop, too.)

Clinton also has the very nice McLain Rogers public park, with a swimming pool and water slides, at the center of town along 10th Street (old Route 66), next to the Route 66 Miniature Golf Course.

For food, west of town along the I-40 frontage, just north of exit 62, **Jiggs Smoke House** (580/323-5641) is a tiny cabin selling barbecue sandwiches but specializing in travel-friendly beef jerky. Alas, Clinton's longtime favorite Route 66 restaurant, Pop Hick's, burned to the ground in 1999, with no insurance and no real chance of being rebuilt. Another blast froom the past, Elvis Presley, stayed at least four times at the **Tradewinds Inn** ($50 and up; 580/323-2610), across from the Route 66 museum at 2128 Gary Boulevard. Elvis's room has been "preserved" as a mini shrine, and you can stay in it (for around $100) and experience a time warp back to the mid-1960s.

Elk City

The last—or first, depending on your direction—sizeable town east of the Texas border, **Elk City** (pop. 10,510, "Home of Suzanne Powell, Miss America 1981") was a popular stopover on Route 66, as evidenced by the many old motels along the various alignments of the old highway through town. Long before Elk City had its Route 66 heyday, it was a wild frontier town along the cattle trails from Texas to Dodge City, Kansas. The area's cowboy and pioneer history is recounted in the **Old Town Museum** (daily; $5; 580/225-6266), on the far west side of town, where there's a re-created Wild West town, complete with doctor's office, schoolhouse, tepee, and rodeo museum. A newer addition to Old Town Museum is the official **National Route 66 Museum,** which has a HUGE Route 66 shield outside; inside there's an old pickup truck decorated to look like the one from *The Grapes of Wrath,* and lots of other old road–related memorabilia.

During the 1940s oil and gas were discovered underground, and the town experienced another short boom, a time remembered by the towering "Rig 114," a record-breaking, 180-foot-tall drilling rig, installed after its retirement in the park next to the Casa Grande Hotel, at 107 E. 3rd Street.

Elk City has two more surefire Route 66 attractions: excellent, Okie-style onion burgers at **Billy's,** 210 N. Madison (580/225-3355), and the delectable French Silk Pie (butter, sugar and vanilla served in a graham cracker crust) baked at the **Country Dove Tea Room,** 610 W. 3rd Street (580/225-7028).

Sayre

If you want a quick flashback to the dark days of Steinbeck's *The Grapes of Wrath,* turn north off I-40 into sleepy **Sayre** (pop. 4,114). The landmark Beckham County Courthouse, which looms over the east end of Main Street, was prominently featured in the movie version as Henry Fonda and the rest of the Joads rattled down Route 66 toward California. The Depression era also lives on in the cool and pleasant WPA-era swimming pool in Sayre City Park, in between the old Route 66 alignments. Just off the old road, take a look in the ever-expanding **Shortgrass Country Museum** (hours vary; free), housed in the old Rock Island Line railroad depot at 106 E. Poplar Street, with changing displays documenting regional history from Cheyenne times to the arrival of homesteading settlers

Just east of the Texas/ Oklahoma border, **Texola** has dried up and all but blown away since it was bypassed by I-40, but a few remnants still stand, awaiting nostalgic photographers. The only signs of life hereabouts are the shouts and swears emanating from the combination pool hall and beer bar housed in the large metal shed on the south side of the old highway, where you're welcome to watch the most passionate domino games this side of Yuma, Arizona.

In Jack D. Rittenhouse's original **A Guide Book to Highway 66,** published in 1946 and now widely available in reprinted versions, he described Erick as "the first town you encounter, going west, which has any of the true 'western' look, with its wide, sun-baked street, frequent horsemen, occasional sidewalk awnings, and similar touches." His description still rings true today.

Welcome to Texola.

during the great Land Rush of 1892. East of the museum stands a giant grain elevator that has rusted into a gorgeous orange glow.

To savor Sayre's Route 66 charm, stay the night at the **Western Motel,** 315 NE Highway 66 ($50 and up; 580/928-3353), which has a fine old neon sign.

Erick

Along with main streets named for local musical heroes Sheb "Purple People Eater" Wooley and Roger "King of the Road" Miller, **Erick** (pop. 1,083) has another unique draw: the **100th Meridian Museum** (hours vary; 580/526-3221), on Route 66 at the only stoplight in town. Displays inside trace life on what used to be considered the edge of the habitable world—everything west of the 100th Meridian was officially thought to be the "Great American Desert"—and also explain that Erick used to be on the Texas border, until the border was realigned. Yet more old stuff is on show a block south at the pack-ratting Harley-rider heaven **Sand Hills Curiosity Shop**, and back on Route 66, be sure to check out the small new **Roger Miller Museum,** established by the widow of the original "King of the Road."

A mile south of the I-40 freeway, a nice stretch of late-model Route 66 continues west from Erick as a four-lane divided highway, all the way to Texas through the borderline ghost town of Texola.

TEXAS

Known as the Panhandle because of the way it juts north from the rest of Texas, this part of the route is a nearly 200-mile stretch of pancake-flat plains. Almost devoid of trees or other features, the western half, stretching into New Mexico, is also known as the Llano Estacado or "Staked Plains," possibly because early travelers marked their route by driving stakes into the earth. The Texas Panhandle was the southern extent of the buffalo-rich grasslands of the Great Plains, populated by roving bands of Kiowa and Comanche Indians as recently as 100 years ago. Now oil and gas production, as well as trucking and Route 66 tourism, have joined ranching as the region's economic basis.

Even more so than in New Mexico or Oklahoma, old Route 66 has been replaced by I-40 most of the way across Texas, though in many of the ghostly towns like McLean, Shamrock, or Vega, and the sole city, Amarillo, old US-66 survives as the main business strip, lined by the empty remains of roadside businesses. A select few are still open for a cup of coffee and a sharp taste of the living past.

McLean

Founded around the turn of the 20th century by an English rancher, Alfred Rowe, who later lost his life on the *Titanic* in 1912, **McLean** (pop. 830) is now perhaps the most evocative town along the Texas stretch of Route 66. Bypassed only in the early 1980s, the old main drag is eerily silent, with a few businesses—a barber shop, a boot shop, and some motels, including one with a fine Texas-shaped neon sign—holding on despite the drop in passing trade.

East of McLean along the old Route 66 frontage, north of the freeway near exit 148, a skeletal sign still spells out the command:
"Rattlesnakes Exit Here."

McLean is headquarters of the state's Historic Route 66 Association, and efforts are being made to preserve the town in prime condition, which explains the lovingly restored Phillips 66 station at 1st and Gray Streets (on the westbound stretch of old Route 66—the pumps price gas at 19 cents a gallon!), and the many other

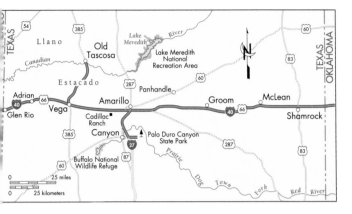

odds and ends on display around town. The center of activity here is the wonderful **Devil's Rope Museum** (daily; free; 806/779-2225), at 100 S. Kingsley Street at the east end of downtown, which has a huge room full of barbed wire—the "Devil's Rope"—and some of the most entertaining and educational collections of Route 66 memorabilia you'll find anywhere. No hype, just lots of good stuff and friendly people telling you all about it.

Groom

The town of **Groom** (pop. 587), 40 miles east of Amarillo on the north side of I-40 at exit 113, holds two of the more eye-catching sights along old Route 66. One of these is a water tower that leans like the Tower of Pisa, causing drivers to stop and rub their eyes, then stop and pull out the camera to take some snapshots to show the folks back home. The other landmark is even harder to miss, a gigantic stainless steel cross (19 stories tall and weighing nearly three tons, this was the largest cross in the Western hemisphere until a copycat erect-

ed a slightly taller one along I-70 in Effingham, Illinois), erected by a religious group in 1995 and just shy of 200 feet tall.

Amarillo

At the heart of the Llano Estacado, midway across the Texas Panhandle, **Amarillo** (pop. 185,000; yes, you pronounce the "l"s) is a busy, big city that retains its cowboy roots. Center of the local ranching industry that handles some two million head of cattle each year, Amarillo handles nearly 90 percent of all the beef in Texas and some 25 percent of the national total.

Most of the Texas Panhandle's 20 inches of **annual rain** falls during summer thunderstorms that sweep across the plains between May and August.

Amarillo is also one of the few places on earth where **helium** has been found; an estimated 90 percent of the world's supply once came from here, but local supplies have been exhausted.

Old Route 66 followed 6th Street through Amarillo, past the brick-paved streets of the Old San Jacinto district around Western Avenue, where you can wander amongst ancient-looking gun and saddle shops, numerous Wild West–themed clothing shops, and kitsch-minded antique shops. To eat and drink with the Coors-drinking cowboys and cowgirls of Amarillo, head west to the **Golden Light Cafe** (806/374-9237), at 2908 W. 6th Avenue, a fairly funky roadhouse famed for burgers, homemade hot sauce, green-chile stew, and Frito pies. Amarillo is best known for its many good steakhouses, the most famous of which has to be the 450-seat **Big Texan Steak Ranch,** which started in 1960 along historic Route 66 and now stands on the east side of Amarillo, off I-40 exit 74, marked by a false-front Wild West town and a giant cowboy atop a billboard. This is the place where they offer a free 72-ounce steak, provided you eat it all—plus a table full of salad, baked potato, and dessert—in under an hour. If you don't finish everything, the cost is around $55; regular meals and very good "normal" steaks are available as well.

There's a nice motel featuring a Texas-shaped swimming pool at the **Big Texan** ($40 and up; 806/372-5000), and dozens of moderate chain motels stand along the I-40 and I-27 frontages, so rooms shouldn't be hard to find.

Palo Duro Canyon State Park

Lovely **Palo Duro Canyon,** one of the most beautiful places in all Texas, is just 25 miles southeast of Amarillo, east of the town of Canyon off the I-27 freeway. Cut into the Texas plain by the Prairie Dog Fork of the Red River, Palo Duro stretches for over 100 miles, with canyon walls climbing to over 1,200 feet.

Cadillac Ranch

No, you're not seeing things—there really are nearly a dozen Cadillacs upended in the Texas plain west of Amarillo, roughly midway between Chicago and Los Angeles. Two hundred yards south of I-40 between the Hope Road and Arnot Road exits (numbers 62 and 60, respectively), some six miles west of Amarillo where old US-66 rejoins the interstate, the rusting hulks of 10 classic Caddies are buried nose-down in the dirt, their up-ended tail fins tracing design changes from 1949 to 1964.

A popular shrine to America's love of the open road, Cadillac Ranch was created by the San Francisco–based Ant Farm artists' and architects' collective in May 1974, under the patronage of the eccentric Amarillo helium millionaire Stanley Marsh 3. The cars were all bought, some running, some not, from local junkyards and used car lots at an average cost of $200 each. Before the Cadillacs were planted, all the hubcaps and wheels were welded on, a good idea since most of the time the cars are in a badly vandalized state. Every once in a while advertising agencies and rock bands tidy them up for use as backdrops during photo shoots. In August 1997, the Cadillacs got another 15 minutes of fame when Marsh decided to dig them up and move them a mile west from where they'd been—to escape the ever-expanding Amarillo sprawl and preserve the natural horizon.

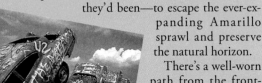

There's a well-worn path from the frontage road if you want a closer look, and visitors are allowed any time, day or night.

Coronado and company were the first Europeans to lay eyes on the area, and numerous Plains tribes, including Apache, Kiowa, and Comanche, later took refuge here. From the end of Hwy-217, a well-paved road winds past the Palo Duro park visitors center (daily; 806/488-2227), from where a short trail leads to a canyon overlook. Beyond here the road drops down into the canyon and follows the river on a 15-mile loop trip through the canyon's heart. It's prettiest in spring and fall, and fairly popular year-round.

On your way to or from Palo Duro Canyon, be sure to stop by the excellent **Panhandle-Plains Historical Museum** (daily; $7; 806/651-2244), at 2401 4th Avenue in the neighboring town of Canyon. One of the state's great museums, this has extensive exhibits on the cultural and economic life of the Panhandle region and its relations with Mexico, the Texas Republic, and the United States. The museum, which is housed in a WPA-era building on the campus of West Texas A&M University, has a special section on rancher Charles Goodnight (1836–1929), who once owned a half million acres here, invented the "chuckwagon," and was an early advocate of saving the bison from extinction.

Vega and Adrian: Midpoint Cafe

Between Amarillo and the New Mexico border, the landscape is identical to what lies east of the city: endless flat plains dotted with occasional oil derricks and Aermotor windmills. The one biggish town, **Vega** (pop. 950), has a very photogenic collection of former and still-functioning businesses, including **Roark Hardware** at 214 S. Main Street ("The Oldest on Route 66"), the Hickory Café (806/267-2569) at the center of town, and a nicely preserved 1920s "Magnolia" service station.

West of Vega, the main event hereabouts is both a geographical and culinary magnet: the hamlet of **Adrian**

(pop. 150) and the unmissable **Midpoint Cafe** (daily March–Jan.; 806/538-6379). One of the route's most enjoyable places to eat, located more or less at the halfway point in

Route 66's long ride between Chicago and Los Angeles—both of which are 1,139 miles away—the Midpoint is friendly, has great food, and basically epitomizes all that old-fashioned hospitality that makes Route 66 such a special experience. Be sure to check out the fine selection of Route 66 books and "Midpoint" souvenirs, or just stop by for a piece of baked-from-scratch "Ugly Crust" pie. As more than one satisfied customer has said, you can taste the happiness.

NEW MEXICO

Following old Route 66 across New Mexico gives you a great taste of the Land of Enchantment, as the state calls itself on its license plates. There is less of the actual "old road" here than in other places, but the many towns and ghost towns along I-40, built more or less on top of Route 66, still stand. Route 66 runs around the historic heart of the state's cultural and political capital, **Santa Fe,** and right through the heart of its sprawling Sun Belt commercial center **Albuquerque,,** while in other places finding the old road and bypassed towns can take some time, though the effort is usually well rewarded.

Western New Mexico has the most to see and the most interesting topography, with sandstone mesas looming in the foreground and high, pine-forested peaks rising in the distance. Paralleling the Santa Fe Railroad, the route passes through the heart of this region, and numerous detours—to **Inscription Rock** and **Chaco Canyon,** among others—make unforgettable stops along the way. In the east, the land is flatter and the landscape drier as the road transitions from the Great Plains.

The border between Texas and New Mexico marks the boundary between **Central** and **Mountain time zones.** Set your clocks and watches accordingly.

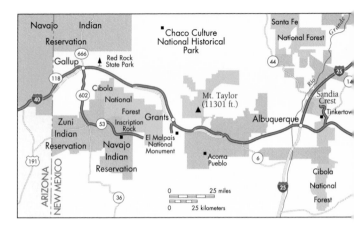

Tucumcari

Subject of one of the most successful advertising campaigns in Route 66's long history of roadside hype, **Tucumcari** (pop. 5,989) looks and sounds like a much bigger place than it is. Also known as "the town that's two blocks wide and two miles long" (though Tucumcari Boulevard, which follows the route blazed by old Route 66 through town, stretches for closer to seven miles between Interstate exits), Tucumcari does have a little of everything, including a great range of neon signs, but it can be hard to explain the attraction of the town that hundreds of signs along the highways once trumpeted as Tucumcari Tonite—2,000 Motel Rooms. (A new ad campaign plays on this legacy, but signs now say Tucumcari Tonite—1,200 Motel Rooms.)

Hype or no hype, Tucumcari is a handy place to break a journey, and even if you think you can make it to the next town, you will never regret stopping here for a night. Especially if you stop at the famous **Blue Swallow Motel** ($55 and up; 505/461-9849), at 815 E. Tucumcari Boulevard, which no less an authority than *Smithsonian* magazine called "the last, best, and friendliest of the old-time motels." Thanks to the warm hospitality of former owner Lillian Redman, few who stayed there during her long reign would

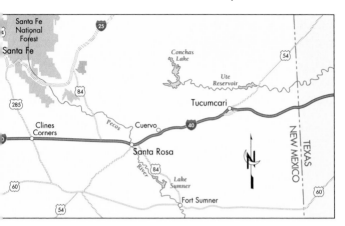

Buddy Holly, Clovis Man

South of Tucumcari, at the edge of the desolate Llano Estacado that stretches south and east across the Texas Panhandle, the city of Clovis is a large railroad and ranching town that has two unique claims to fame. One is that it was the site where some of the oldest archaeological remains ever found in North America were unearthed: In the 1930s, archaeologists dug up bones and arrowheads that proved human habitation dating back as early as 9000 BC. Some of these artifacts, belonging to what archaeologists have dubbed "Clovis Man," are on display at the **Blackwater Draw Museum** (daily; $2; 505/562-2202), on US-70 about 10 miles south of Clovis.

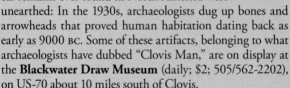

Clovis is also semi-famous for having played a part in early rock 'n' roll: Buddy Holly came here from Lubbock, across the Texas border, in the late 1950s to record "Peggy Sue," "That'll Be The Day," and other early classics. You can tour the restored Norman Petty studios, located at 1313 W. 7th Street but open only by appointment (505/763-3435).

disagree, and the new owners (Terri and Bill Kinder) have kept up the old spirit while improving the plumbing and replacing the mattresses. Each room comes with its own garage, and the neon sign alone is worth staying awake for.

Across Route 66 from the Blue Swallow stands another survivor, the landmark tepee fronting the historic **Tee Pee Trading Post** (505/461-3773) at 924 E. Tucumcari Drive, where friendly owners Mike and Betty Callens will tempt you to add to your collection of Southwest or Route 66 souvenirs (or "Damn Fine Stuff," as their business cards have it). For a place to eat, try the Mexican food at **La Cita** (505/461-0949), under the turquoise and pink sombrero on the corner of 1st Street and old Route 66.

A trio of newer additions fill out Tucumcari's roster of attractions: one is a chromed steel **Route 66 sculpture,** welcoming travelers at the west edge of town; another is the vivid Route 66 mural painted on the corner of 2nd Street. The third is the **Mesalands Dinosaur Museum** ($5; 505/461-3466), a block north of Route 66 at 211 E. Laughlin Street. Housed inside Mesa Technical College, the museum boasts "the largest collection of life-sized bronze prehistoric skeletons in the world," plus real fossils, unusual minerals, and the unique *Torvosaurus,* a very rare carnivorous cousin of legendary *Tyrannosaurus rex.*

Santa Rosa

The I-40 freeway has bisected the town of **Santa Rosa** (pop. 2,744) and cut its old Route 66 frontage in two, but for over 65 years, travelers crossing New Mexico along Route 66 and I-40 made a point of stopping here for a meal at Club Cafe, "The Original Route 66 Restaurant Since 1935." Thanks to signs lining the road for miles in both directions, emblazoned with the smiling face of the "Fat Man," the Club Cafe became nationally famous for its always-fresh food. The Club Cafe closed in 1992, but its legacy (and the Fat Man logo) live on at **Joseph's,** 865 Will Rogers Drive (505/472-1234), which has a nifty neon sign and very good food at reasonable prices on old Route 66, a half mile southwest of I-40 exit 275.

On the opposite side of Route 66 from

Along the Pecos River via US-84, some 50 miles southeast of Santa Rosa, the gravesite of Wild West legend Billy the Kid lies outside the town of **Fort Sumner.** The grave is part of a private museum (daily; $2) adjacent to Fort Sumner, where 7,000 Navajo people were imprisoned from 1864 to 1869.

Joseph's, marked by a bright yellow hot rod atop a 30-foot pole, the **Route 66 Auto Museum** (505/472-1966), at 2766 W. Route 66, has a wide-ranging exhibit on "anything to do with wheels," highlighted by some tricked-out old Fords and Chevys and a totally cherry 1957 T-Bird convertible.

Santa Rosa's other main attraction is unique: the **Blue Hole,** an 80-foot-wide, 240-foot-deep artesian well filled with water so crystal-clear that it draws scuba-divers from all over the western states to practice their underwater techniques here. The water of the Blue Hole, at around 61°F, is too cold for casual swimming, but in the summer heat it's a great place to cool your heels. The Blue Hole is well signed at the end of Blue Hole Road, a half mile south of old Route 66.

East of Santa Rosa, along the south side of I-40, one of the oldest stretches of Route 66 is only partly paved, and best done in a 4WD or on a mountain bike. Here you get an indelible sense of what travel was like in the very early days, when less than half the route's 2,400-odd

Along I-40 near Cuervo, Ricardo Montalban narrates a brief, State of New Mexico–sponsored history of Route 66 on **530 AM.**

miles were paved. Another stretch of old (circa 1926–1935) Route 66, off Blue Hole Road just south of the "official" Historic Route 66, now lies underneath the runway of Santa Rosa's small airport.

Tinkertown and the Sandia Crest

Not that there's any shortage of wacky roadside Americana along what's left of Route 66, but one of the most endearing of them all, **Tinkertown** (daily; $3; 505/281-5233), is a quick 10-minute drive north of the old road. Like an old-fashioned penny arcade run riot, Tinkertown is a marvelous assembly of over a thousand delicately carved miniature wooden figures, arranged in tiny stage sets to act out animated scenes—a circus Big Top complete with side show, a Wild West town with dance-hall girls and a squawking vulture—all housed in a ramshackle building made in part out of glass bottles and bicycle wheels, created over the

Clines Corners, midway between Albuquerque and Santa Rosa off I-40 exit 218, is a truck stop café that dates back to 1934 and is, as the signs say, Worth Waiting For–for the huge gift shop if not for the unexciting food.

past 50-odd years by Ross and Carla Ward and family. It's impossible to describe the many odds and ends on show here—one display case holds over 100 plastic figures taken from the tops of wedding cakes, for example—especially since the whole thing is always being improved and "tinkered" with, but the spirit of the place is aptly summed up in the Tinkertown motto: "We Did All This While You Were Watching TV." The Dalai Lama loved it, and so will you.

To get to Tinkertown, turn off I-40 at exit 175, six miles east of Albuquerque, and follow Hwy-14 for six miles, toward Sandia Crest. Tinkertown is on Hwy-536, 1.5 miles west of the Hwy-14 junction, hidden off the highway among the juniper trees.

Albuquerque was also the home of the great travel writer and WW II war correspondent **Ernie Pyle.** His old house, at 900 Girard Avenue, a half mile south of Central Avenue, is now the city's oldest public library, which includes his collected works and a few personal items in a small display.

Sandia Crest itself is another 12 miles uphill at the end of Hwy-536 National Scenic Byway; the ridge offers a phenomenal panorama from an elevation of 10,678 feet. Back on Hwy-14, south of Tinkertown some four miles north of I-40, the **Sandia Mountain Hostel,** 12234 N. Hwy-14 in Tijeras (505/281-4117), offers clean bunks in a ski- and bike-friendly environment.

Albuquerque

Roughly located at the center of New Mexico, the sprawling city of **Albuquerque** (pop. 463,300) spreads north and south along the banks of the Rio Grande and east to the foothills of 10,000-foot Sandia Crest. By far the state's biggest city, Albuquerque is a young, energetic, and vibrantly multicultural community, which, among many features, boasts a great stretch of old Route 66 along Central Avenue through the heart of the city—18 miles of diners, motels, and sparkling neon signs. For an offbeat taste of the city's Route 66 heritage, keep an eye out for the remarkable **Aztec Motel** (505/254-1742), at 3821 Central Avenue, a very funky Pueblo-style 1930s motel kept alive as a live-in sculpture gallery and artists' community.

One of the best parts of town is **Old Town,** the historic heart of Albuquerque. Located a block north of Central Avenue, at the west end of Route 66's cruise through downtown, Old Town offers a quick taste of New Mexico's Spanish colonial past, with a lovely old church, the 300-year-old **San Felipe de Neri,** as well as shops and restaurants set around a leafy green park. An information booth in the park has walking-tour maps of Old Town and other information about the city. Another Old Town attraction, one that carries on the Route 66 tradition of reptile farms and private zoos, is the **Rattlesnake Museum** (daily; $2.50), southeast of the main square at 202 San Felipe Street, where you can see a range of rattlers from tiny babies to full-sized diamondbacks, about 50 all together, plus fellow desert-dwellers like tarantulas and a giant Gila monster.

Though most people associate computer giant **Microsoft** with Seattle, the company actually began here in Albuquerque in 1975, in a series of dingy Route 66 motels.

New Mexico's long relationship with radioactivity is reflected in the name of Albuquerque's very popular Florida Marlins–affiliated Class AAA baseball club, the **Isotopes** (505/924-2255), who play just south of downtown. Games are broadcast on **KNML 610 AM.**

A very different look into New Mexico's varied cultural makeup is offered at the **Indian Pueblo Cultural Center** (daily; $6; 505/843-7270), a block north of I-40 exit 158 at 2401 12th Street. The center is owned and operated by the state's 19 different Pueblo communities; its highlight is a fine museum tracing the history of the region's Native American cultures, from Anasazi times up to the Pueblo Revolt of 1680, with the contemporary era illustrated by video presentations and a mock-up of a typical tourist—camera, shorts, and all. On most weekends ceremonial dances are held in the central courtyard—free and open to the general public. There's also a small cafeteria where you can sample food like fry bread and Navajo tacos, and a smoke shop selling discount cigarettes.

Downtown Albuquerque has been under reconstruction seemingly forever, with an ambitious mixed-use project surrounding the train station and massive old Santa Fe Railroad yards. The state has pledged money for it, so someday soon the area may feature the enticing-sounding **Wheels Museum,** 1501 SW 1st Street (505/243-6269), tracing (surprise, surprise . . .) transportation in New Mexico, from covered wagons on the Santa Fe Trail through the heyday of railroads and Route 66.

Albuquerque Practicalities

The largest city in New Mexico, Albuquerque makes a very handy point of entry for tours of the Southwestern United

Santa Fe

New Mexico's state capital, and one of the prime vacation destinations in the country, Santa Fe has been at the center of Southwest life for centuries and at the cultural crossroads of a region that has been settled for thousands of years. From the east, detour north from Clines Corners via US-285, or for the full "Historic Route 66" tour follow US-84 north near Santa Rosa toward Las Vegas (the original one, here in New Mexico), then continue west on I-25, parallel to the pioneer-era Santa Fe Trail.

Despite its swirling hordes of vacationers, and its vast infrastructure of hotels, restaurants, art galleries, and souvenir shops, Santa Fe remains one of the most enjoyably un-American small cities. It makes the most sense to begin your tour of Santa Fe at its center, the **Plaza.** This will help you get not only your geographical bearings but also a historical context with which to appreciate the rest of Santa Fe. On the north side of the Plaza, the **Palace of the Governors** (closed Mon.; $8), is the oldest public building in America. Dating from 1610, the palace served as residence for Spanish, Mexican, and, later, American territorial governors until 1909, when the New Mexico legislature voted to turn the building into the Museum of New Mexico. The museum contains an excellent overview of the building's and the city's tumultuous history, numerous artifacts and documents, and an exhaustive collection of regional photographs.

To get a sense of the life and work of the woman who did as much as anyone to fix Santa Fe in the American mind, walk two blocks west from the Plaza to the **Georgia O'Keeffe Museum,** 217 Johnson Street (daily; $8; 505/946-1038), which displays more than 120 pieces of the late artist's work. Many of the paintings here depict the landscape in and around her home at Abiquiu, north of Santa Fe, where she lived for 40 years.

Shops, shops, and more shops (plus a few cafés and restaurants) line the streets emanating from the Plaza. Many of these have a decidedly upscale bent; there are about 250 art galleries alone in Santa Fe, for instance (though the most engaging and scenic stretch of them is found along narrow and tree-lined Canyon Road, which runs east from Paseo de Peralta up into the foothills above town). Once you penetrate Santa Fe's Paseo de Peralta, the historic ring road encircling the 17th-century city center, leave your car at one of the many parking lots or garages and see Santa Fe on foot. Another downtown street, Old Pecos Trail, carried Route 66 for its first dozen years before Santa Fe was bypassed in favor of Albuquerque in 1937.

After you've done the downtown tour, hop in the car and cruise south along the Old Santa Fe Trail (past the Zia Indian–inspired **state capitol** building) and up a hill to what is known as Museum Plaza, a compound comprising two more of the Museum of New Mexico sites, plus the **Wheelwright Museum of the American Indian,** which presents traditional Indian arts and crafts.

If you're interested in classical music, the **Santa Fe Chamber Music Festival** (505/983-2075) performances take place in July and August in a variety of atmospheric old Santa Fe buildings.

Practicalities

It's a pleasant surprise that only moderately deep pockets are needed to find good food or memorable accommodations in Santa Fe. With recipes that show the influence of more than 2,000 years of Native American culture (which contributed three major staples: beans, corn, and squash), some 400 years of Catholic inclusion (chiles, cilantro, cumin, onions, garlic, wheat, rice, and both beef and pork), and a liberal dash of American inventiveness, Santa Fe restaurants serve the world's oldest, newest, and, some say, tastiest cuisines—often all side by side on the very same plates. Menu offerings include dishes like a buttermilk corn cake with smoky chipotle-chile shrimp (and a side of red chile onion rings), *chile rellenos* stuffed with roast duck and black bean mole sauce, or blue corn turkey enchiladas, mean Santa Fe's fine food is at least as much a draw as its rich history and magical mountain light.

To ease your way into Santa Fe food, start on the Plaza at the **Plaza Restaurant,** at 54 Lincoln Avenue (505/982-1664), which has been serving no-nonsense meals since it opened in 1918. Part of the fun here is the constant clatter of dishes and silverware, the old-fashioned tile floor, and a rear wall with a giant mural map of the Southwest. If you don't have time for a full meal (the New Mexico meatloaf is a specialty), pop in for a helping of **Frito pie,** which is quite the local delicacy (although the recipe allegedly originated in Texas in the 1930s, when Daisy Doolin, the mother of the Dallas-based founder of Frito-Lay, poured chili over her Fritos and found that she liked it).

Tecolote Cafe

Another outstanding source of filling New Mexican breakfast fare is **Tecolote Cafe,** a mile southwest of the Plaza at 1203 Cerrillos Road (505/988-1362). Closer in, and well worth a visit for its addictive breakfast quesadilla (with scrambled eggs, applewood-smoked bacon, Jack cheese, and guacamole), is **Cafe Pasqual's,** just off the Plaza at 121 Don Gaspar Avenue (505/983-9340), which has deliciously inventive dishes at lunch and dinner, too.

After a meal elsewhere (unless someone else is paying your expenses!), join Santa Fe's old guard at the **Pink Adobe** (also called simply "The Pink"), 406 Old Santa Fe Trail (505/983-7712), a very deluxe, retro-minded supper club that's also home to the kitschy Dragon Room bar, a popular late-night hangout.

For a convenient and memorable place to stay, a pair of small B&B gems are within a short walk of the Plaza: **Adobe Abode,** 202 Chapelle Street ($150 and up; 505/983-3133), and the **Casa del Toro,** 229 McKenzie Street ($125 and up; 505/820-6177. The former, as the name suggests, consists of several large adobe-style rooms and casitas, and both have modern baths, upscale amenities, and eclectic antiques and folk furnishings.

If you prefer to park within sight of your room, there's a nice motor inn, with a location that's hard to beat: **Garretts Desert Inn,** a block off the plaza at 311 Old Santa Fe Trail ($95 and up; 505/982-1851). If all the desirable places are full, or if you're tight on funds, cruise along busy Cerrillos Road (Hwy-14), where you'll find all the major chains.

For complete listings of accommodation options, and for information on anything else to do with Santa Fe, contact the **Santa Fe Convention and Visitors Bureau,** 60 E. San Francisco Street (505/955-6200 or 800/777-2489).

States. For old-road fans, the best stretch of Route 66 through Albuquerque is probably the section along Nob Hill, east of downtown and Old Town near the University of New Mexico. Here you'll find vintage neon and some great places to eat and drink, including **Kelly's Brew Pub** (505/262-2739), housed in a 1930s Streamline Moderne auto dealership at 3222 E. Central Avenue; and the upscale **Monte Vista Fire Station** (505/255-2424), at 3201 E. Central Avenue. Between Nob Hill and downtown, the excellent **Route 66 Diner** (505/247-1421), at 1405 E. Central Avenue, serves top-quality burgers and shakes, and regional specialties like blue-corn pancakes.

Another good range of places to eat lies within walking distance of Old Town. Enjoy a delicious mix of Mexican and American diner food at **Garcia's** (505/842-0273), at 1736 W. Central Avenue, beneath a glorious neon sign. For a taste of 1950s Americana (and good root beer), head to the **Route 66 Malt Shop,** housed in an old gas station and motor court at 1720 W. Central Avenue (505/242-7866). Another old Route 66 landmark, **Mac's La Sierra** (505/836-1212), serves up "Steak in the Rough" and other beefy specialties in a cozy, dark wood dining room a long ways west of town at 6217 W. Central Avenue.

Like most of New Mexico, Albuquerque has a ton of inexpensive accommodations, with all the usual chain motels represented near the airport and along the Interstate frontage roads, plus a lot of fading or extinguished old stars of the Route 66 era, like the famous El Vado, 2500 W. Central Avenue, which has been threatened with demolition for decades. For Route 66 character, consider: the still neat and tidy, Del Webb–built **Hiway House Motel,** in the Nob Hill district at 3200 E. Central Avenue ($65 and up; 505/268-5113), or the unimaginatively but accurately named **Monterey Non-Smokers Motel,** near Old Town at 2402 W. Central Avenue (around $75; 505/243-3554). Since its 2008 renovation, the nicest old hotel has got to be the grand **La Posada** ($150 and up; 505/242-9090), a block off old Route 66 at 125 2nd Street downtown, one of the first inns built by New Mexico–born hotel magnate Conrad Hilton.

Old Route 66: Bernalillo

True fans of the full of the Route 66 tour, and anyone interested in the art and architecture (and food!) of the American Southwest, will want to make the detour to the state capital, Santa Fe. The original Route 66 alignment ran north from Albuquerque along the I-25 corridor, then curved back south from Santa Fe, along what's now US-84, to rejoin I-40 west of Santa Rosa.

The best sense of this old route across old New Mexico comes just north of Albuquerque, at the historic town of **Bernalillo.** Route 66 here follows the much older El Camino Real, which linked these Spanish colonies 400 years ago. The heart of Bernalillo contains two great stops, poles apart from each other in ambience but together capturing the essence of the place. First of these is ancient-feeling **Silva's Saloon** (505/867-9976) at 955 Camino del Pueblo, whose walls, coated in layers of newspaper clippings, old snapshots, and other mementos form a fabulously funky backdrop for a cold beer, a burger, or an evening listening to local live music alongside cowboys, bikers, and other characters. Up the street is the stylish **Range Cafe** (505/867-1700), at 925 S. Camino del Pueblo, where a spacious dining room has very good "New New Mexican" food (try the bread pudding!) and a sophisticated, big-city air.

Rio Puerco and the Route 66 Casino

Between Albuquerque and Acoma Pueblo, a fine old stretch of old Route 66 survives, passing crumbling tourist courts and service stations across the Laguna Indian Reservation. The photogenic Route 66 highlight here is the graceful old steel truss **Rio Puerco Bridge,** which spans a usually dry river, right alongside the I-40 superslab about 10 miles west of Albuquerque. The old road ambience is also overwhelmed by the huge new **Route 66 Casino,** south of the freeway, the largest of many gambling complexes that have sprung up on Indian reservations across this part of New Mexico. Besides the jinglingly huge, 50,000-square-foot casino (which has the usual card tables, craps, and roulette), the complex also has a 2,800-seat theater, a roadside café, a smoke shop offering cheap (tax-free) tobacco, and a large hotel ($80 and up; 505/352-STAY or 866/711-STAY).

The heart of the historic Laguna Pueblo, where some 500 people live in adobe buildings around a church that dates from 1699, is not really open to travelers, but just west of the pueblo the old Route 66 frontage runs past an old road land-mark: **Budville,** where the remnants of an old trading post and café still stand in atmospheric silence along the south side of the highway.

Acoma Pueblo: Sky City

A dozen miles east of Grants and 50 miles west of Albuquerque, one of the Southwest's most intriguing sites, **Acoma Pueblo,** stands atop a 350-foot-high sandstone mesa. Long known as "Sky City," Acoma is one of the very oldest communities in North America, inhabited since AD 1150. The views out across the plains are unforgettable, especially toward Enchanted Mesa on the horizon to the northeast.

> Broadcasting on **530 AM** around the Acoma area, actor **Ricardo Montalban** narrates the story of the pueblo's conquest by the Spanish, and the story of the building of San Esteban church high atop the mesa.

Few people live on the mesa today, though the many adobe houses are used by Pueblo craftspeople, who live down below but come up to the mesa-top to sell their pottery and other crafts to tourists. To visit this amazing place, you have to join a guided **tour** (daily; $12; 800/747-0181), which begin with a bus ride to the mesa-top and end with a visit to **San Esteban del Rey Mission,** the largest Spanish colonial church in the state. Built in 1629, the church features a roof constructed of huge timbers that were carried from the top of Mt. Taylor on the backs of neophyte Indians—a distance of more than 30 miles.

Acoma Pueblo is 15 miles south of I-40, from exit 108 (west-bound) or exit 96 (eastbound). Start your visit by appreciating the artifacts displayed in the beautiful new **Haak'u Museum,** at the base of the mesa, where tours of the ancient Sky City begin. The Acoma tribe also operates the money-spinning **Sky City Casino and Hotel** (1-888/SKY-CITY), sited well away from the historic core of the pueblo, right off I-40 exit 102.

Pie Town and the Lightning Field

A long way south of Grants, an old mining camp was so fa-mous for fine desserts it became known as **Pie Town.** After many years of pielessness, local meringue-lovers lucked out when baker Kathy Knapp opened the **Pie-O-Neer Cafe** (505/772-2711), on old US-60 at milepost 59.

East of Pie Town off US-60, the **Lightning Field** (May–Oct. only; 505/898-3335) is an outdoor "land art" installation by Walter De Maria, who implanted a grid of steel tubes into the New Mexico plain with the intention of attracting lightning strikes. The sculpture consists of 400 stainless steel poles situated in a rectangular grid roughly one mile by one kilometer; the engineering feat here was to set the poles so that their tops form an exactly level plane. For the full Lightning Field experience, you have to stay overnight in nearby cabin, and meals and transportation to the site are included in the $150 to $250 per person fees. The Lightning Field is maintained by the same foundation that curates the intriguing DIA-Beacon museum, north of New York City.

Grants

Along with the usual Route 66 range of funky motels and rusty neon signs, the former mining boomtown of **Grants** has the unique attraction of the **New Mexico Mining Museum** (closed Sun; $3; 505/287-4802), right downtown on old Route 66 (Santa Fe Avenue) at the corner of Iron Avenue. Most of the exhibits trace the short history of local uranium mining, which began in 1950 when a local Navajo rancher, Paddy Martinez, discovered an odd yellow rock that turned out to be high-grade uranium ore. Mines around Grants once produced half the ore mined in the United States, but production has ceased (pending renewed interest in nuclear power . . .). From the main gallery, ride the elevator down (only one floor, but it feels like 900 feet) to the highlight of the mining museum: a credible re-creation of a uranium mine, complete with an underground lunch room emblazoned with all manner of warning signs.

Midway between Grants and Gallup, I-40 crosses the 7,250-foot **Continental Divide,** where the Top O' the World dance hall used to tempt travelers off old Route 66. From here (exit 47), it's possible to follow the old road for 30 miles, running east along I-40 as far as Grants.

If you're lucky, the **Uranium Cafe** will still be in business across the street from the Mining Museum; just look for the atomic neon sign, a rarely lit Route 66 landmark.

Inscription Rock and El Malpais: Hwy-53

Western New Mexico is among the most beautiful places on the planet. South of I-40 and Route 66, one of the best drives through it, Hwy-53, loops between Gallup and Grants across the Zuni and Navajo Nation Indian Reservations. Skirting the southern foothills of the 9,000-foot Zuni Mountains, along the edge of the massive **El Malpais** lava flow—thousands of acres of pitch-black, concrete-hard, glassy sharp rock sliced and diced by lava tubes and collapsing craters. Formed between 10,000 and 115,000 years ago, most of the Malpais is wild and undeveloped, but on the slopes of Bandera Volcano, you can tour the privately run **Ice Cave** (daily; $9; 505/783-4303), where the cool temperatures are very welcome on a hot summer's day.

West from El Malpais, the route follows ancient Indian trails that Coronado used on his ill-fated 1540 explorations, winding past piñon-covered hills, open grasslands, and the fascinating graffiti collection of El Morro National Monument. Better known as **Inscription Rock,** the 200-foot-high sandstone cliffs of El Morro have been inscribed by travelers like Juan de Oñate, who wrote his name with a flourish in 1605, after he "discovered" the Gulf of California.

Atop the cliffs are the partially excavated remains of a small pueblo dating from around AD 1200. A two-mile loop trail to the inscriptions and the ruins starts from a small **visitors center** (daily; $4 per car; 505/783-4226), where exhibits outline the history of the site. The trails are closed an hour before sunset, so get here early enough in the day to enjoy the beautiful scenery. There is also a small campground (no showers, pit toilets) amidst the junipers.

Much less developed, but every bit as memorable as the cliff dwellings of Mesa Verde, the extensive archaeological remains protected inside **Chaco Culture National Historical Park** are well worth your time. Though it's an hour's drive from I-40 via unpaved roads, the park is one of the wonders of the Southwest desert.

Southwest of Inscription Rock, animal lovers may want to visit the **Wild Spirit Wolf Sanctuary** (closed Mon.; $5; 505/775-3304), where over a dozen wolves and wolf-dogs live on a 100-year-old moonshiner's ranch.

Gallup

Though it's not exactly scenic, **Gallup** (pop. 20,209) is a fascinating place. Founded in 1881 when the Santa Fe Railroad first rumbled through, and calling itself "The

Gallup also hosts the annual **Inter Tribal Ceremonial,** perhaps the largest Native American gathering in the country, held early in August at Red Rock State Park, eight miles east of Gallup, and culminating in a Sunday parade that brings some 30,000 people out to line old Route 66 through town. Festivities include a rodeo, powwows, and a beauty show; call for the latest details (505/836-3896).

Gateway to Indian Country" because it's the largest town near the huge Navajo and other Native American reservations of the Four Corners region, Gallup has some of the Southwest's largest trading posts and one of the best strips of neon signs you'll see anywhere on old Route 66.

For travelers intent on experiencing a little of the charms of old Route 66, Gallup also has **El Rancho** ($50 and up; 505/863-9311), at 1000 E. Route 66, a delightful old hotel lovingly preserved in its 1930s glory. Built by a brother of movie director D. W. Griffiths, El Rancho feels like a national park lodge, with a large but welcoming lobby dominated by a huge stone fireplace. All the rooms in the old wing are named for the movie stars who have stayed here over the years—the W. C. Fields Room, the John Wayne Room, the Marx Brothers Room (which sleeps six), even the Ronald Reagan Room— and signed glossies of these and many more actors and actresses adorn the halls. El Rancho also has a good restaurant serving regional food, and a gift shop selling souvenirs and locally crafted jewelry, pottery, and rugs.

In the heart of historic downtown, the old Santa Fe train depot (still in use by Amtrak), houses the **Gallup Cultural Center** (505/863-4131) at 201 E. Route 66; free dance shows are staged here nightly in summer, next to a statue of a WW II Navajo Code Talker. Another place worth spending some time is **Richardson's Cash Pawn and Trading Post** (505/722-4762), at 222 W. Route 66. Family run since 1913, this busy but friendly space is crammed to the rafters with arts, crafts, and pawned goods—Navajo rugs and jewelry, ornately tooled leather saddles, pearl-inlaid guitars, and more—that give a better sense of local lifestyles (and all their ups and downs) than any museum ever could.

ARIZONA

If you're not yet a die-hard Route 66 fan, traveling the old route across Arizona is bound to convert you. The high-speed I-40

freeway gives quick access to some of the best surviving stretches of the old road, and these are some of the most captivating parts of Route 66 anywhere. Between the red-rock mesas of New Mexico and the arid desert along the Colorado River, the route runs past dozens of remarkable old highway towns along some of the oldest and longest still-driveable stretches of the Mother Road.

East of Flagstaff, the old road is effectively submerged beneath the freeway, which drops down to cross desolate desert, passing through desiccated towns and **Petrified Forest National Park.** Remnants of numerous old roadside attractions—Indian trading posts, wild animal menageries, and Holbrook's famous "Sleep in a Teepee" Wigwam Village—all survive in varying degrees of preservation along Arizona's section of Route 66.

Midway across the state, the route climbs onto the forested (and often snowy) Kaibab Plateau for a look at the mighty **Grand Canyon,** one of the true wonders of the natural world.

Painted Desert and Petrified Forest National Park

Right along the New Mexico border, Arizona welcomes westbound travelers with an overwhelming display of trading-post tackiness—huge concrete tepees stand at the foot of brilliant red-rock mesas, while gift shops hawk their souvenirs to passing travelers. The gift shops themselves may not be all that attractive, but the old Route 66 frontage road along here, a.k.a. Hwy-118 between exit 8 in New Mexico and exit 357 in Arizona, is truly spectacular, running at the foot of red-rock cliffs. If you like rocks, gems, and petrified wood, a fine collection is for sale at the endearingly strange **Stewart's Trading Post,** marked by a family of animated dinosaurs at I-40 exit 303.

Oddball kitsch aside, the easternmost 60 miles of I-40 across Arizona are little more than one long speedway, since almost any sign of the old road has been lost beneath the four-lane interstate.

I-40 and old Route 66 trace the southern edge of the massive **Navajo Nation Indian Reservation,** home of the nation's most populous tribe and of radio station **KTNN 660 AM,** which broadcasts a fascinating mélange of Navajo chants and Jimi Hendrix riffs on a "clear" signal that (especially at night) reaches all over the western USA. KTNN is also the only station in the United States that broadcasts pro football games—in Navajo.

One place that's worth a stop here is **Petrified Forest National Park** (daily dawn–dusk; $10 per car; 928/524-6228). The polished petrified wood on display in the visitors center is gorgeous to look at but seeing 93,000 acres of the stuff in its raw natural state is not, to be honest, particularly thrilling. The story of how the wood got petrified is interesting, though: About 225 million years ago, a forest was buried in volcanic ash, then slowly embalmed with silica and effectively turned to stone. Alongside the visitors center at the entrance to the park, there's a handy restaurant and a gas station.

While the park contains a vast array of prehistoric fossils and pictographs as well as the petrified wood, one of the more interesting sights is the old **Painted Desert Inn,** a Route 66 landmark during the 1920s and 1930s that was converted into a museum and bookstore after the Park Service took it over in the 1960s. The pueblo-style building, now restored to its 1920s splendor with lovely murals, Navajo rugs and sand paintings, and handcrafted furnishings, is perched on a plateau overlooking the spectacularly colored **Painted Desert** that stretches off toward the northern horizon.

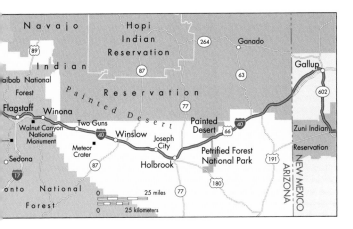

Holbrook: Wigwam Village

Holding a concentrated dose of old Route 66 character, **Holbrook** (pop. 4,917) is definitely worth a quick detour off the I-40 freeway. More than the other Route 66 towns in the eastern half of Arizona, it still feels like a real place, with lively cafés and some endearing roadside attractions around the center of town, where Route 66 alternates between Hopi Drive and Navajo Boulevard. Along with the many rock shops—be sure to check out the huge dinosaur collection outside the **Rainbow Rock Shop,** a block south on Navajo Boulevard near the railroad tracks—and trading post tourist traps, another worthwhile place to stop is the **Navajo County Museum** (closed Sun.; free) in the old Navajo County Courthouse, four blocks south of I-40 at the corner of Navajo Boulevard (old Route 66) and Arizona Street. The collections are wide-ranging and include a walk downstairs to the old county jail, in use from 1899 until 1976 (the graffiti is great).

In and around Holbrook, you'll come across a series of concrete dinosaurs rescued from the old **International Petrified Forest Dinosaur Park,** which used to stand along I-40 near exit 289.

A great introduction to the Four Corners region, the **Hubbell Trading Post National Historic Site** (928/755-3254), 38 miles north of I-40 from exit 333 and a mile west of the town of Ganado, is a frontier store preserved as it was in the 1870s, when trader John Hubbell began buying the beautiful rugs made by local Navajo weavers.

Best of all, stop for the night at the marvelous **Wigwam Village** (around $55; 928/524-3048), at 811 W. Hopi Drive at the western edge of town, and sleep in a concrete tepee. Based on the original circa-1936 Wigwam Village motor

West of Holbrook along I-40, Joseph City is noteworthy for two things. East of town, the giant 1000MW Cholla power plant consumes more than 100 tons of coal every hour. At the west end of town, on the south side of I-40 at exit 269, there's the **Jackrabbit Trading Post,** the one whose signs you've probably noticed over the past hundred miles—take a picture or buy a postcard of the giant jackrabbit, one of a long line of creatures who have stood here since 1949.

court built in Cave City, Kentucky, Holbrook's was one of seven franchises across the country; this one opened in 1950 but closed down when the Interstate came through in 1974. The family of original owner Chester Lewis fully renovated the buildings and reopened the place after his death in 1988; original bentwood hickory furniture, a small curio shop, and a handful of historic American cars parked outside help complete the ambience of classic roadside Americana. Especially if you want to introduce the younger generations to the joys of old-road travel, you really should stay here at least once in your life.

After you've checked in to the Wigwam, be sure to wander down the road for a friendly, filling Route 66 meal at **Joe and Aggie's Cafe** (928/524-6540) at 120 W. Hopi Drive, or **Romo's Cafe** (928/524-2153) across the street.

Winslow

Winslow, Arizona, didn't make it into Bobby Troup's original Route 66 hit list, but the town more than made it a generation later when the Eagles recorded the Jackson Browne tune "Take It Easy," which begins, "Standin' on a corner in Winslow, Arizona," a line that has caused more people to turn off in search of the place than anything else.

In between I-40 and Route 66, the funky **Old Trails Museum** (Tues.–Sat.; 520/289-5861), at 212 Kinsley Street, sells a range of "Standin' on the Corner" T-shirts and displays a few reminders of Winslow in its heyday. Down the fire-damaged block, on 2nd and Kinsley, where a little sign stakes a claim to being *the* corner the Eagles sang about, there's a statue of a guy with a guitar, and a mural of a girl (my lord!) driving by in a flatbed Ford, slowing down to take a look.

The usual chain motels and fast-food franchises stand at either end of town around Winslow's I-40 exits, but in between is a great landmark of Southwest style: the elegant **La Posada Hotel** ($125 and up; 928/289-4366) at 303 E. 2nd Street. Designed in the late 1920s for Fred Harvey by architect Mary Colter, who considered it her masterpiece, the hotel was closed for 40 years before being fully and lovingly restored and reopened in 1998. Near a busy rail line but surrounded by very pleasant gardens, the luxurious hotel is also home to a stylish cocktail bar and one of the finest restaurants for miles, the Turquoise Room. If you have the time and inclination to appreciate its old-fashioned, handcrafted charms, La Posada is an unforgettable stop.

Meteor Crater

Between Winslow and Winona, three miles east of Two Guns and six miles south of I-40 exit 239, sits **Meteor Crater** (daily; $12; 928/289-2362), Arizona's second-most-distinctive hole in the ground. Formed by a meteorite some 50,000 years ago and measuring 550 feet deep and nearly a mile across, the crater is a privately owned tourist attraction. The Astronauts Hall of Fame plays up the crater's resemblance to the surface of the moon (Apollo moon-walkers practiced here). You can't climb down into it, but (weather permitting) you can join a guided rim tour, walking a half mile there and back across the desert to gaze down into the crater.

Back along I-40, at the exit for Meteor Crater, the **Meteor City Trading Post** boasts the usual range of souvenirs plus "The World's Largest Map of Route 66." Stretching 100 feet from end to end, the mural/map was originally created by noted Route 66 artist Bob Waldmire, but after fading and flaking it was "restored" by volunteers and the Hampton Inn motel chain back in 2002.

Two Guns and Twin Arrows

Heading west from Meteor Crater toward Flagstaff, the route climbs swiftly from the hot red desert up into the cool green pines, but old-road fanatics will want to take the time to explore what remains of two old-time tourist traps lining the next 20 miles of highway. Keep your eyes peeled approaching I-40 exit 230: the freeway crosses deep Diablo Canyon, where an old Route 66 bridge still spans the dry wash, and the walls of a half dozen bleached buildings are all that's left of the **Two Guns Trading Post.** A roadside attraction par excellence, Two Guns had a zoo full of roadrunners,

Songs of Route 66

If you ever plan to motor west,

Travel my way, that's the highway that's the best,

Get your kicks on Route 66.

It winds from Chicago to L.A.,

More than 2,000 miles all the way,

Get your kicks on Route 66.

Now you go through St. Looey, Joplin, Missouri,

And Oklahoma City is mighty pretty.

You'll see Amarillo, Gallup, New Mexico, Flagstaff,
Arizona, don't forget Winona, Kingman, Barstow,
San Bernardino.

Won't you get hip to this timely tip:

When you make that California trip,

Get your kicks on Route 66.

Get your kicks on Route 66.

—Bobby Troup

Gila monsters, and coyotes, and one building still has a sign saying Mountain Lions—all for the entertainment of passing travelers. According to various reports down the Route 66 grapevine, Two Guns has been on the verge of reopening in recent years, but most of the time the old road is blocked by a sign reading No Trespassing by Order of Two Guns Sheriff Department. Probably a good thing, since the old buildings are all dangerously close to collapse. It's an evocative site, nonetheless, and photogenic in the right light.

A dozen miles west of Two Guns is another bilateral attraction: **Twin Arrows,** where a pair of giant but decaying red arrows point toward a long-closed café, right off the freeway at exit 219.

Don't Forget: Winona

East of Flagstaff, in fact across most of eastern Arizona, follow-

One of the most popular road songs ever written, and a prime force behind the international popularity of Route 66, "Get Your Kicks on Route 66" was penned by jazz musician Bobby Troup in 1946 while he was driving west to seek fame and fortune in Los Angeles. Troup consistently credited his former wife Cynthia, with whom he was traveling, for the half dozen words of the title and refrain. The rest of the song simply rattled off the rhyming place-names along the way, but despite its apparent simplicity, it caught the ear of Nat King Cole, who made it into a hit record and also established the pronunciation as "root" rather than "rout," as repeated in later renditions by everyone from Bob Wills to the Rolling Stones.

If you haven't heard the song for a while, there's a jazzy version by Bobby Troup, along with some lively Route 66–related songs, on the compilation CD, *The Songs of Route 66—Music from the All-American Highway,* available at souvenir stores en route.

ing old Route 66 can be a frustrating task, since much of the roadway is blocked, discontinuous, torn up, or all three. Unlike the long stretches found in the western half of the state, here the old road exists only as short segments running through towns, and most of the way you're forced to follow the freeway, stopping at exit after exit to get on and off the old road. Among the places worth considering is the one town mentioned out of sequence in the Route 66 song: "Flagstaff, Arizona, don't forget Winona," which, alas, is now little more than a name on the sign at I-40 exit 211.

Walnut Canyon National Monument

The most easily accessible of the hundreds of different prehistoric settlements all over the southwestern United States, **Walnut Canyon National Monument** (daily 8 AM–4 PM, 7 AM–5 PM in summer; $5; 928/526-3367) is also one of the prettiest places imaginable, with piñon pines and junipers clinging to the canyon walls, and walnut trees filling the canyon floor. On the edge of the canyon, a small visitors center gives the historical background, but the real interest lies below, on the short but very steep Island Trail that winds through cliff dwellings tucked into overhangs and ledges 400 feet above the canyon floor. Storms in early 2008 dislodged a huge boulder that crashed down and wiped out part of the trail, so check with the rangers to make sure the trail is open, and ask about weather, water supplies, and other safety issues. The rim of Walnut Canyon is nearly 7,000 feet above sea level, and the altitude makes the climbing especially strenuous.

The entrance to the Walnut Canyon monument, which contains some 300 identified archaeological sites, lies seven miles east of Flagstaff, accessible from I-40 exit 204.

Flagstaff

An old railroad and lumber-mill town given a new lease on life by an influx of students at Northern Arizona University, and by the usual array of ski bums and mountain bikers attracted by the surrounding high mountain wilderness, **Flagstaff** (pop. 52,894) is an enjoyable, energetic town high up on the Coconino Plateau. The natural beauty of its forested location has meant that, compared to other Route 66 towns, Flagstaff was less affected by the demise of the old road. That said, it still takes pride in the past, notably in the form of the **Museum Club** (928/526-9434), at 3404 E. Route 66, an old roadhouse brought back to life as a country-western nightclub and ad-hoc nostalgia museum.

Along with a great but slowly shrinking range of classic neon signs, Flagstaff also has a pair of non–Route 66 related attractions. First and foremost of these stands high on a hill on the west side of downtown Flagstaff, reachable from the west end of Santa Fe Avenue (old Route 66): the **Lowell Observatory,** established in 1894 by Percival Lowell and best known as the place where, in 1930, the onetime planet Pluto was discovered. A **visitors center** (daily in sum-

Way back in 1945, in his classic *A Guide Book to Highway 66,* Jack Rittenhouse wrote that "Cowboys and Indians can be seen in their picturesque dress on Flagstaff streets year-round . . .," but these days he'd probably notice the lycra-clad cyclists who crowd into the college town's many cafés.

Flagstaff's **San Francisco Street** was named not for the California city but for the nearby volcanic peaks, so called by early Spanish missionaries and still held sacred by the native Hopi Indians.

mer, $6; 928/774-3358) has descriptions of the science behind what goes on here—spectroscopy, red shifts, and expanding universes, for example—and the old telescope, a 24-inch refractor, is open for viewings 8–10 PM most nights in summer. Not exactly consistent with its neon-lit Route 66 reputation, Flagstaff has since the 1950s been a pioneer in combating light pollution; to help preserve the dark sky at night, here at the observatory and also at the surrounding natural sights, Flagstaff has proclaimed itself the world's first (and so far only) "International Dark Sky City."

Flagstaff's other main draw, the **Museum of Northern Arizona** (daily; $5; 928/774-5213), perches at the edge of a pine-forested canyon three miles northwest of downtown via US-180, the main road to the Grand Canyon; extensive exhibits detail the vibrant cultures of northern Arizona, from prehistoric Puebloans to contemporary Hopi, Navajo, and Zuni.

Flagstaff very nearly became an early movie center, when young **Cecil B. DeMille** stopped here briefly while scouting locations to shoot the world's first feature-length film, a Western called *The Squaw Man*. It was snowing in Flagstaff that day, so he moved on to Los Angeles.

Downtown Flagstaff has more than enough espresso bars—probably a dozen within a two-block radius of the train station—to satisfy its many multiply pierced, twenty-something residents. There are also ethnic restaurants specializing in Greek, Thai, German, or Indian cuisine, so finding suitable places to eat and drink will not be a problem. For breakfast and lunch, it's hard to beat this great pair: **Kathy's** (928/774-1951), a cozy café at 7 N. San Francisco Street, across from **MartAnne's Burrito Palace,** serving delicately deep-fried *chimichangas* at 10 N. San Francisco Street (928/773-4701).

Accommodations, too, are plentiful, and you can pick either the motel with the most appealing sign (try the **Western Hills,** 1580 E. Route 66, 928/774-2152), or step back into an even earlier time and stay at the classy railroad-era **Hotel Monte Vista** ($65–130; 928/779-6971 or 800/545-3068), right off old Route 66 at 100 N. San Francisco Street. It was good enough for Gary Cooper, and it has been restored to its Roaring '20s splendor.

Sunset Crater and the Grand Canyon

While 90 percent of visitors approach the Grand Canyon from the south, a better and less crowded approach follows US-89 and Hwy-64, climbing up from the Navajo Nation deserts onto the Kaibab Plateau. The views are amazing in any direction—north across the desiccated Colorado Plateau, east across the colorful Painted Desert, west to the forests of the Kaibab Plateau, or south to the angular San Francisco Peaks, including 12,663-foot Mount Humphreys, the highest point in Arizona.

Cameron is named in memory of a cantankerous prospector-turned-early-promoter of the Grand Canyon. **Ralph Cameron** blazed the Bright Angel Trail (then charged tourists $1 to use it) and did everything he could to obstruct the government from taking over "his" canyon—even going so far as to get elected U.S. senator (in 1920) so he could try to eliminate the newly established national park.

This route is somewhat longer than the US-180 route to the Grand Canyon, but in most other ways it's far superior—not least because it gives access to a huge variety of scenery and historic sites. The first of these, 12 miles north of Flagstaff and three miles east of US-89, is **Sunset Crater** a 1,000-foot-tall black basalt cone tinged with streaks of oranges and reds and capped by a sulfur-yellow rim—hence the name, which was bestowed by explorer John Wesley Powell in 1892. You can hike through the lava field that surrounds the cone, but the cone itself is off limits.

Sunset Crater marks the start of a scenic loop that winds around for some 30 miles through neighboring Wupatki National Monument (daily; $3; 928/679-2365). The monument protects the remains of a prehistoric Native American community, thought to have been ancestors of the Hopi, who lived here between 1100 and 1225 AD and now inhabit the broad mesas rising to the northeast. Hundreds of ruins—most in very fine condition—are spread over the 35,000-acre monument. The largest ruin, 100-room **Tall House,** stands near a ceremonial amphitheater and a very rare ball court, which may indicate a link with the Mayan cultures of Central America.

Back on US-89, 20 miles north of the north entrance to Wupatki, the crossroads settlement of Cameron stands at the

Grand Canyon National Park (continued)

12-mile round-trip from the South Rim. If you can finagle a reservation, you can extend the stay (and delay the climb back up) by staying overnight at Phantom Ranch, another three miles from Plateau Point on the north side of the Colorado River, which is traversed by a pair of suspension bridges. Nearby **Bright Angel Campground** has space for more than 100 people, but reservations and a backcountry camping permit are required; call the main visitors center for details.

Another interesting old trail drops down from Grandview Point to Horseshoe Mesa, where you can still see the remnants of an old copper mine that closed in 1907. This is a six-mile round-trip and gives an unforgettable introduction to the Grand Canyon.

No matter where you go, when hiking down into the canyon remember that it will take you twice as long to hike back up again, that the rim can be covered in snow and ice as late as June, and *always carry water*—especially in summer—at least a quart for every hour you're on the trail. The very good **visitors center** (520/638-7888) in Grand Canyon Village has information about the park's many hiking trails, the canyon's geology, the burro rides that take you down and back up again, and anything else to do with the Grand Canyon.

Practicalities

It may give a sense of the immensity of the Grand Canyon to know that, while the North Rim is a mere 6–10 miles from the South Rim as the crow flies, to get there by road requires a drive of at least 215 miles.

Most of what you'll need to know to enjoy your Grand Canyon visit is contained in the brochure you're given at the entrance, where you pay the $20-per-car fee (Golden Eagle and other passes are accepted).

To make advance reservations for accommodations—a good idea at any time of year but essential in the peak summer months—phone the park concessionaire, **Xanterra** (888/297-2757 in advance, 928/638-3283 same-day), which

junction with Hwy-64, which heads up (and up) to the east entrance of Grand Canyon National Park. A mile north of the Hwy-64 junction, along the south bank of the Little Colorado River, historic **Cameron Trading Post** (which also has a $120-a-night motel and an RV park; 520/679-2231) stands next to an equally historic one-lane suspension bridge, built in 1911 (and now carrying an oil pipeline). Cameron makes a good alternative to Tusayan, in case all the Grand Canyon's in-park accommodations are full.

From Cameron, Hwy-64 runs west along the Little Colorado River Gorge, which Hopi cosmology considers to be the place where man emerged into the present world. This deep canyon leads into the much larger Grand Canyon, while Hwy-64 climbs up the plateau for 30 miles to the east entrance of Grand Canyon National Park. Your first overlook is a desert view, where the photogenic 1930s Watchtower gives a great taste of the canyon from the highest point on the South Rim.

Williams

The last Route 66 town to be bypassed by I-40, **Williams** (pop. 2,842; elev. 6,780 ft) held out until the bitter end, waging court battle after court battle before finally surrendering on October 13, 1984. Despite the town's long opposition, in the end Williams gave in gracefully, going so far as to hold a celebration-cum-wake for the old road, highlighted by a performance atop a new freeway overpass by none other than Mr. Route 66 himself, Bobby "Get Your Kicks" Troup.

Williams today is primarily a gateway to the Grand Canyon, but it also takes full tourist advantage of its Route 66 heritage: The downtown streets sport old-fashioned street lamps, and every other store sells a variety of Route 66 souvenirs, making the town much more than a pit stop for Grand Canyon–bound travelers. Apart from the Route 66 connections, Williams's pride and joy is the vintage **Grand Canyon Railway,** which whistles and steams its way north to the canyon every morning March–December, taking roughly two hours each way. Call for current schedules and fares (round-trip costs around $60; 800/843-8724), or stop by the historic depot, a former Harvey House hotel restored in 1990.

For an easy way to wake up, enjoy fresh pastries and a great

Grand Canyon National Park

One of the wonders of the natural world, the Grand Canyon of the Colorado River—two hundred miles long, a mile deep, and anywhere from five to 15 miles across—defies description, and if you're anywhere nearby you really owe it to yourself to stop for a look. The most amazing thing about the Grand Canyon, apart from its sheer size and incredible variety of shapes and colors, is how different it looks when viewed from different places (artist David Hockney has said that the Grand Canyon is the only place on Earth that makes you want to look in all directions—up, down, and side to side—at the same time), so be sure to check it out from as many angles, and at as many different times of day, as you can. A book like this one can do little more than hint at all there is to see and do, but if you have time for nothing else, take a quick hike down into the canyon to get a real sense of its truly awesome scale.

The great majority of the more than five million people who visit the Grand Canyon each year arrive at the South Rim and gaze down into the Grand Canyon from Mather Point, where the entrance road hits the edge of the gorge. The park visitors center and most of the food and lodging are located a mile west at Grand Canyon Village. Beyond Grand Canyon Village, West Rim Drive winds west, leading past the J. W. Powell Memorial at Hopi Point (from where you get great views of the Colorado River, which otherwise can be surprisingly hard to see) and a series of other view fore ending up at Hermit's Rest, eight miles fr Canyon Village—where there are yet more stupen as well as restrooms, drinking fountains, and a gift

The **West Rim Drive,** which was built for t the Santa Fe Railroad in 1912, is closed to cars out summer, but frequent shuttle buses stop viewpoints. A seven-mile hiking trail runs west Powell Memorial to Hermit's Rest, and a th paved nature trail links the Powell Memorial wi Canyon Village.

East from Mather Point, **East Rim Drive** ru miles, stopping first at aptly named Grandview miles from Grand Canyon Village and a half m of the East Rim Drive. This is, literally and fig a high point of any Grand Canyon tour, giving a gree panorama over the entire gorge. Continu the road passes a small prehistoric pueblo at Ruins before ending with a bang at **Dese Watchtower,** an Anasazi-style tower set right at of the canyon. Though it looks ancient, the to created for tourists in 1932, designed by Mary also the architect of the Bright Angel Lodge and the wonderful old Harvey House hotels that line 66 across the Southwest.

From the watchtower, the road continues along through the east entrance, then drops down to th roads town of Cameron and the Little Colorado R

Grand Canyon Hikes

To get a real feel for the Grand Canyon, you get out of the car, get beyond the often overcr viewpoints that line the South Rim, and take down into the depths of the canyon itself. Th popular and best-maintained path, the **Bright Trail,** descends from the west end of Grand C Village, following a route blazed by prospectors 1890s. It's an all-day, 17-mile hike down t Colorado River and back, but there are rest (with water) along the way. A shorter day hike c to **Plateau Point,** 1,300 feet above the river

(continued on nex

NV AZ · Lake Mead National Recreation Area · Grand Canyon · Hualapai NP · Grand Canyon Skywalk Reservation · Peach Springs 66 · Indian Reservation · Supai · Havasupai Indian Reservation · Kaibab National Forest · Grand Canyon · Colorado River · UTAH / ARIZONA · ALT 89 · 89 · 67 · Canyon National Park · Navajo Indian Reservation · Kaibab National Forest · Tusayan · 180 · 64 · 89 · 160 · 0 25 miles · 0 25 kilometers

handles reservations for the six very different lodges in Grand Canyon Village. The most characterful and best-value place to stay is the **Bright Angel Lodge,** which overlooks the canyon; the cheapest rooms share bathrooms, while others have canyon views and fireplaces. The coffee shop here is open all day, there's a pretty nifty soda fountain right on the edge of the canyon, and the lobby fireplace shows off the rock strata, in proper chronological order, that form the walls of the Grand Canyon. The other historic lodge is the **El Tovar Hotel,** built in 1905 but recently renovated; rooms here start around $150 and top out at more than $300 a night. The El Tovar also has the park's best restaurant—and a comfy piano bar to help while away the night.

For a basic motel bed, there are four other lodges in Grand Canyon Village, offering more than 750 rooms altogether, costing $75–125 a night. There's also a very nice lodge at the North Rim, open in summer only.

It's more of an effort to reach, but the best place to get a feel for the Grand Canyon is splendid **Phantom Ranch,** a rustic complex of cabins and dormitories way down in the canyon, on the north side of the Colorado River. Space here is usually taken up by people on overnight burro-ride packages (which cost around $300), but in off-season particularly you may be able to get a bed without the standard six months' (or more) advance reservation. Ask at the desk in the Bright Angel Lodge, or call 928/638-3283.

Reservations for camping (877/444-6777 or online at www.recreation.gov) at the South Rim are also essential in summer. The largest facility, **Mather Campground,** is across from the visitors center and is open year-round, with more than 300 sites (no hookups; $18 a night) and coin-operated showers. A variety of sites with RV hookups are available nearby at the Xanterra-run **Trailer Village** (888/297-2757 in advance, 928/638-2631 same-day). There's another National Park Service campground at Desert View, near the east entrance, and backcountry camping (overnight permits required) is available at established sites down in the canyon.

(continued on next page)

Grand Canyon National Park (continued)

If all the in-park accommodations are full, hundreds of rooms are available in Williams and Flagstaff, and right outside the park's southern boundary at **Tusayan,** where you can choose from a Best Western, a Holiday Inn Express, and a Quality Inn. Tusayan (which has the third-busiest airport in Arizona) is also headquarters for a half dozen companies offering airplane and helicopter tours of the canyon; you can't miss their billboards, but details of prices (think $200 per hour) and trips can be got from operators such as **Papillon** (520/638-2419) or **Grand Canyon Airlines** (520/638-2407).

cup of coffee, cappuccino, or espresso in one of the comfy chairs of **Java Cycle,** 326 W. Route 66 (928/635-1117). If you like pie, you'll want to save time and space for the **Pine Country Restaurant,** serving breakfast, lunch, dinner, and famous fresh pies near the train station at 107 N. Grand Canyon Boulevard (928/635-9718). Williams is also home to a landmark old Route 66 restaurant, **Rod's Steak House** (928/635-2671), at 301 E. Bill Williams Avenue, in business since 1946.

For a place to stay—and there are many, thanks to the nearby Grand Canyon—there are a couple of old motor court motels, one disguised as an **EconoLodge** ($60 and up; 928/635-4085), at 302 E. Route 66, another branded as a **Rodeway** ($85 and up; 928/635-2619). At the upper end of the scale, try the plushly renovated **Lodge on Route 66,** 200 E. Route 66 ($125 and up; 928/635-4534), or look into that historic Harvey House hotel, now known as the **Grand Canyon Railway Hotel** ($125 and up; 928/635-4010), ideal for passengers taking the vintage train to the Grand Canyon.

Sedona and Jerome

Most Arizona visitors head for the Grand Canyon, but smaller and still scenic Oak Creek Canyon, just south of Flagstaff, has one great advantage over its world-famous neighbor: you can drive through it, on scenic Hwy-89A. Starting right at the edge of Flagstaff, this red sandstone gorge has been cut into the surrounding pine and juniper forests by eons of erosion.

The most popular place to enjoy Oak Creek Canyon, **Slide Rock State Park** (520/282-3034), 18 miles south of Flagstaff and seven miles north of Sedona, is a 55-acre, day-use-only area focused on the long, natural rock chute for which the park is named. Nearby **Slide Rock Lodge** (520/282-3531) has peaceful motel rooms starting around $85 in summer. No TVs or Wi-Fi are provided, but there are barbecue grills for the do-it-yourself cook.

At the south end of Oak Creek Canyon, 25 miles from Flagstaff, the otherworldly landscape surrounding Sedona (pop. 16,000) has made it one of the nation's most popular vacation destinations, particularly for New Agey visitors, who in the past 20 years have made Sedona into a upmarket center for psychic channeling, soul travel, and the like. Sedona first came to attention in the 1950s, when the red-rock spires that dominate the local landscape were seen in a wide variety of Hollywood westerns (including *Johnny Guitar*). Despite the rampant sprawl—and the high hotel rates, which can reach $200 a night—Sedona is still well worth a look, especially if you can get away from the town and explore some of the surrounding wilderness.

West from Sedona, Hwy-89A makes a wonderfully scenic drive past 7,743-foot Mingus Mountain into photogenic Jerome (pop. 403; elev. 5,400 feet), the liveliest and most interesting "ghost town" in Arizona. Set on steep streets that switchback up the mountainside, Jerome is an old copper mining camp that has turned itself into a thriving artists' community, with many nice shops, galleries, and cafés, and almost no touristy schlock. Park wherever you can and walk around, enjoying the incredible views out over the Verde Valley to the San Francisco Peaks and beyond.

At the north (uphill) edge of town, a mile off Hwy-89 at the end of fairly rough Perkinsville Road, the **Gold King Mine** (daily 9 AM–5 PM; $3) has a misleading name but is still a great place to go. Not so much a mine as an anarchic collection of ancient-looking machinery (sawmills, pumps, hoists, trucks, cars, and ore cars), most of which is kept in working order), plus an intact old gas station dating from Jerome's 1920s heyday.

At the heart of Jerome, enjoy food or a fine shot of espresso at the **Flatiron Cafe,** 416 Main Street (928/634-2733), or for a full meal with a great view, try the delicious Asylum dining room inside the huge old **Jerome Grand Hotel,** a former hospital at 200 Hill Street ($125 and up; 928/634-8200).

Looping along from Jerome, Hwy-89 runs west then north, rejoining Route 66 at Ash Fork.

Seligman

One of best places to stop and get a feel for the spirit of old Route 66, the sleepy little town of **Seligman** (pop. 510; SLIG-man) is a perfect place to take a break before or after rejoining the Interstate hordes. The town retains a lot of its historic character—old sidewalk awnings and even a few hitching rails—and offers lots of reasons to stop, including Angel Delgadillo, the town barber, whose shop at 217 E. Route 66 is a pilgrimage point for old-roads fans. His brother Juan Delgadillo created and ran the wacky **Snow Cap Drive-In** (928/422-3291) a half block to the east, where the sign says Sorry, We're Open, and the menu advertises Hamburgers without Ham. Behind the restaurant, in snow, rain, or shine, sits a roofless old Chevy decorated with fake flowers and an artificial Christmas tree. Juan died in 2004 (at the ripe old age of 88), but his family carries on the Snow Cap traditions, and the burgers, fries, and milk shakes (not to mention the jokes!) are worth driving miles for.

Between I-40 exit 139, just west of Ash Fork, and the wonderful town of Seligman, a very nice section of the old Route 66 two-lane runs all the way to Seligman along the railroad tracks just north of, and parallel to, the I-40 freeway. Coming into Seligman on this stretch of Route 66, you'll be greeted by the fantastic Rusty Bolt junk shop and oddball emporium, impossible to miss along the north side of the old highway.

Delgadillo's Snow Cap

Seligman, which in

the 1940s was the location of Andreas Feininger's classic Route 66 photograph, also has a very good café, the **Copper Cart** (928/422-3241), at 103 W. Chino Avenue in the center of town. The railroad used to be Seligman's raison d'etre, an era remembered by the neat old mock-Tudor railroad station that once doubled as a Harvey House hotel and restaurant. For an overnight, choose from a half dozen motels (but not the Unique Motel, which is now a sign only) like the nice, clean, and friendly **Historic Route 66 Motel** ($60 and up; 928/422-3204) at 500 W. Route 66.

Probably the most evocative stretch of old Route 66 runs between Seligman and Kingman through the high-desert Hualapai ("WALL-ah-pie") Reservation, along the Santa Fe Railroad tracks through all-but-abandoned towns bypassed by the "modern" Interstate world.

Grand Canyon Caverns

Far, far away from the high-speed freeway frontage, 22 miles northwest of Seligman and a dozen miles east of Peach Springs, a large green sign marks the entrance to **Grand Canyon Caverns** (daily; $12; 928/422-4565), which has somehow managed to survive despite being bypassed by the I-40 superslab. Once one of the prime tourist draws on the Arizona stretch of Route 66, the Grand Canyon Caverns were discovered and developed in the late 1920s and still have the feel of an old-time roadside attraction. Tours start every hour at the gift shop, where you hop on the elevator that drops you 300 feet to underground chambers, including the 18,000-square-foot Chapel of the Ages. Tours last around 45 minutes. There's also a gas station, a motel (with a pool), and a restaurant on the site.

Just west of the Grand Canyon Caverns, Hwy-18 cuts off 65 miles to the northeast toward the Havasupai Indian Reservation, which includes one of the most beautiful and untrammeled corners of the Grand Canyon. No roads, just red rocks, green canyons, cobalt-blue waterfalls, and the **Havasupai Lodge** ($125; 928/488-2111).

Old Route 66 Loop: Grand Canyon Skywalk

Midway along the "Historic Route 66" loop between Seligman and Kingman, the road comes close to the Grand Canyon as it passes through the large and lonely Hualapai Indian Reservation. The 700-strong Hualapai tribe has its community center at the town of **Peach Springs,** which marks the halfway point of this 90-mile, old-roads loop and offers at least

Peach Springs is also the starting point for the 19-mile drive along **Diamond Creek Road—** all the way to the "bottom" of the Grand Canyon. Get a permit and detailed info at the Hualapai Lodge.

one reason to stop: the comfortable **Hualapai Lodge** ($70–115; 928/769-2230) hotel and River Runners restaurant, right on Route 66. Apart from this, Peach Springs is mostly a prefab Bureau of Indian Affairs housing project with few services, though there is a photogenic old Route 66 filling station at the center of town.

The lodge was the first sign of tourism in Peach Springs, but the Hualapai tribe seems to have embraced commerce in a big way: 2007 saw the opening of the much-hyped **Grand Canyon Skywalk,** a glass-floored steel horseshoe that juts out from the edge of the Grand Canyon, 4,000 feet higher than the Colorado River. The very daring and impressive Skywalk is certainly unique, but it's also very expensive (count on $60 per person, including lots of annoying fees and charges to park and ride the bus out to the Skywalk itself). The Skywalk is most popular as a day-trip destination from Las Vegas, but you can get here from Peach Springs via a very rough, 75-mile series of dirt roads—count on driving for at least three hours to get to the Skywalk from just about anywhere (Las Vegas, Kingman, or Peach Springs). The recommended route is to take I-40 or Route 66 as far west as Kingman (50 miles from Peach Springs), then head north via US-93, Pierce Ferry Road, and Diamond Bar Road.

A museum is planned and facilities are being improved as the money rolls in, but for now there isn't much apart from

Old Hackberry Store, HACKBERRY, ARIZONA (ALT. 3,500 FT.)
"IN THIS VIEW FACING NORTH, ACROSS 66, THE RUGGED FOOTHILLS OF THE GRAND WASH CLIFFS FORM A DRAMATIC BACKDROP. THE CLIFFS—WHICH FORM PART OF THE COLORADO PLATEAU'S EDGE—STRETCH AWAY TO THE NORTHWEST, CLEAR TO THE GRAND CANYON.
THE STORE, WITH ITS OUTBUILDINGS & OLD HOUSE, WAS A TYPICAL ROADSIDE OASIS, SERVING TRAVELLERS SINCE THE 1920'S UNTIL THIS STRETCH OF 66 WAS LEFT 'HIGH & DRY' WHEN THE INTERSTATE BYPASSED IT IN 1978.
THE TINY VILLAGE OF HACKBERRY—NAMED FOR TREES AT THE NEARBY HACKBERRY MINE (NORTH, HERE) IS TO THE SOUTH (OUT OF VIEW), JUST BEYOND THE SANTA FE'S DOUBLE TRACKS. BEFORE 66 WAS CONSTRUCTED, TRAFFIC WENT RIGHT THROUGH THE TOWN, ON THE OLD NATIONAL TRAILS ROAD.
THE STORE & ADJACENT PROPERTY WAS PURCHASED IN 1993 BY THE WALDMIRE FAMILY OF ILLINOIS, & PLANS ARE TO ESTABLISH AN 'INTERNATIONAL-BIOREGIONAL OLD ROUTE 66 VISITOR CENTER.'"

HERE 66 IS A 2-LANER, WITH E.-BOUND PASSING LANE.

OLD ROUTE 66 Scenes! ©1992

by R. Waldmire

the Skywalk itself. There's an ambitious plan to develop the entire western end of the Hualapai Reservation into "Grand Canyon West," with all sorts of 4-by-4 jeep tours and outdoor activities on offer; time will tell if the Skywalk can endure once the novelty wears off.

West of Peach Springs, Route 66 winds along the railroad tracks, passing through a few ghost towns (like Hackberry, where the old gas station still stands in rusting splendor), before zooming into Kingman.

Kingman

The only town for miles in any direction since its founding as a railroad center in 1880, **Kingman** (pop. 20,069) has always depended upon passing travelers for its livelihood. Long a main stopping place on Route 66, and still providing the only all-night services on US-93 between Las Vegas and Phoenix, and along I-40 between Flagstaff and Needles, the town remains more a way station than a destination despite the increasing number of people who have relocated here in recent years, attracted by the open space, high desert air, and low cost of living.

The best first stop in Kingman is **The Powerhouse,** 120 West Andy Devine Avenue (928/753-9889), a hulking old power plant that's been inventively reused to house a very good Route 66 museum, with galleries full of enough old cars, postcards, and mementos to occupy you for an hour or more. Best of the bunch is a nifty relief map of the entire path of Route 66 (the many mountain ranges make you realize why old cars needed so many service stations!), and the displays do a good job of evoking and exploring the deep romance many Americans seem to feel for the old Mother Road.

The stretch of Route 66 through Kingman has been renamed in memory of favorite son **Andy Devine,** who was born in Flagstaff in 1905 but grew up here, where his parents ran the Beale Hotel. One of the best-known character actors of Hollywood's classic era, the raspy-voiced Devine usually played a devoted sidekick. Devine's most famous role was as the wagon driver in the classic 1939 John Ford western *Stagecoach;* he also did the voice of Friar Tuck in Disney's version of *Robin Hood* and remained active in films and TV until his death in 1977.

Be sure to contact the **visitors center** here (928/753-6106), to pick up a copy of the town's very good Route 66 brochure, then pop across Route 66 for a burger, some fries, and milk shake at the very good **Mr. D's Route 66 Diner,** at 105 E. Andy Devine Avenue (928/718-0066), impossible to miss thanks to its bank of neon.

Midway between Kingman and Oatman, set against the angular Black Mountains high above the desert plain, **Cool Springs** is a nifty old rough stone service station resurrected as a Route 66 gift shop and mini museum. Built in the 1940s, abandoned in the 1960s, and brought back to life in 2005, Cool Springs is a nice place to stop, buy a soda, and soak up the Route 66 spirit.

The blocks off Route 66 hold Kingman's most interesting older buildings—Beale Street, north of Route 66, has dozens of 100-year-old railroad era storefronts now housing an array of junque and antique shops. Besides the usual chain motels along I-40, accommodation options in Kingman include the pleasant **Hill Top Motel** ($40; 928/753-2198), at 1901 E. Andy Devine Avenue, forever infamous as the place where evil Timothy McVeigh stayed for a week before blowing up the Federal Building in Oklahoma City.

To escape the summer heat, Kingmanites head east and south along a well-marked 14-mile road to **Hualapai Mountain Park,** where pines and firs cover the slopes of the 8,417-foot peak. Hiking trails wind through the wilderness, where there's a campground and a few rustic cabins ($25–65) built by the Civilian Conservation Corps during the New Deal 1930s. Contact the ranger station (928/757-3859) near the park entrance for detailed information or to make reservations.

Old Route 66: Oatman

One of the most demanding, desolate, and awesomely satisfying stretches of the old road loops north from the I-40 freeway, between Kingman and the California border. Climbing over steep mountains while cutting across a stretch of desert that brings new meaning to the word "harsh," the narrow roadway passes few signs of life on this 50-mile loop, so be sure you and your car are prepared for the rigors of desert driving.

Westbound drivers have it the easiest—simply follow the well-signed Historic Route 66 west from Kingman, exit 44 off

Just east of Oatman, old Route 66 passes recently reactivated gold workings while climbing up and over the angular **Black Mountains.** Steep switchbacks and 15-mph hairpin turns carry the old road on a breathtaking 2,100-foot change in elevation over a very short eight miles of blacktop.

I-40. From the west heading east, take Exit 1 on the Arizona side of the river, then head north. Whichever way you go, you can't avoid the steep hills that lead to **Oatman** (elev. 2,700 feet), an odd mix of ghost town and tourist draw that's one of the top stops along Route 66. A gold mining town whose glory days had long faded by the time I-40 passed it by way back in 1952, Oatman looks like a Wild West stage set, but it's the real thing—awnings over the plank sidewalks, bearded rough-necks (and a few burros) wandering the streets, lots of rust, and slumping old buildings. The gold mines here produced some two million ounces from their start in 1904 until they panned out in the mid-1930s; at its peak, Oatman had a population of over 10,000, with 20 saloons lining the three-block Main Street. One of these, the old **Oatman Hotel** (928/768-4408), at 181 N. Main Street, was where Clark Gable and Carole Lombard spent their first night after get-ting married in Kingman in 1939. You can sample Oatman's highly recommended Navajo tacos, have a beer in the down-stairs bar (which is thickly wallpapered in years' and years' worth of dollar bills!), or peer through a Plexiglas door at the room where Clark and Carole slept, hardly changed for half a century.

Crossing the Colorado River between Arizona and California, look downstream (south) from the I-40 freeway to see the arching silver steel bridge that carried Route 66 up until 1966. It's still in use, supporting a natural gas pipeline; beyond it, the red-rock spires for which Needles is named rise sharply out of the desert plains.

Saloons and T-shirt shops line the rest of Main Street, where on weekends and holidays Wild West enthusiasts act out the shootouts that took place here only in the movies. Oatman does get a considerable tourist trade, but after dark and outside of the peak summer tourist season, the town reverts to its rough-and-tumble ways, and the conservative, libertarian bent of most of the local population ensures that nothing is likely to change Oatman's crusty charms.

Lake Havasu City and London Bridge

The first stop east of the Colorado River, nine miles from the border and 23 miles south of I-40, **Lake Havasu City** is a thoroughly modern vacation town built around a thoroughly odd centerpiece: **London Bridge,** brought here stone by stone between 1967 and 1971. Terribly tacky souvenir shops and faux London pubs congregate around the foot of the bridge, which spans a man-made channel to a large island, but the bridge itself is an impressive sight.

The crossing over the Colorado River at the California/Arizona border was the site of illegal but effective roadblocks during the Dust Bowl era, when vigilante mobs turned back migrant Okies if they didn't have much money.

Unless you plan to retire here—or simply rent a houseboat and relax on the water—there's not a lot to do at Lake Havasu. That said, the area has become a popular spring break destination for

London Bridge

It may not have stood out as the finest piece of engineering art when it spanned the Thames, but London Bridge is a marvelous sight in the middle of the Arizona desert. A replacement for a series of bridges that date back to medieval times, inspiring the children's rhyme, "London Bridge Is Falling Down," this version of London Bridge was constructed in the 1830s. When it was no longer able to handle the demands of London traffic, the old bridge was replaced by a modern concrete span and its stones were put up for sale in 1967.

Bought by property developer Robert McCulloch for $2.4 million, the 10,246 blocks of stone were shipped here and reassembled at a cost of another $3 million. After a channel was cut under the bridge to bring water from the Colorado River, the Lord Mayor of London flew in to attend the re-dedication ceremonies in October 1971; the bridge now stands as the centerpiece of a retirement and resort community that's home to some 25,000 residents. There's no admission charge to see this oddly compelling sight, its finely carved stonework standing in permanent rebuke to the tacky stucco, mock-Tudor souvenir shops lining the base of the bridge.

western college kids, thousands of whom flock to **Lake Havasu State Park** (928/855-2784) for fun-in-the-sun and who-knows-what after dark. For the rest of us—have an English muffin and a cup of tea, pay your respects and take a photograph or two, then hit the road again.

CALIFORNIA

From the demanding Mojave Desert, over mountains and through lush inland valleys, to the beautiful beaches of Santa

Monica, Route 66 passes through every type of Southern California landscape. The old road, which survives intact almost all the way across the state, is marked for most of its 315 miles by signs declaring it Historic Route 66. Across the Mojave Desert the route is also marked as the National Old Trails Highway, its title before the national numbering system was put into effect in the late 1920s.

Needles

Founded soon after the Santa Fe Railroad came through in 1883 and named for the group of sharp stone spires that stand near where I-40 crosses the Colorado River from Arizona, **Needles** (pop. 4,830) is one of the hottest places in the country, with summertime highs hovering between 100°F and 120°F for months on end. Though unbearable in summer, Needles is a popular place with winter snowbirds escaping colder climes; it also has a very rich Route 66 heritage. The stretch of old Route 66 through Needles runs along Broadway, alternating along both sides of the freeway. The magnificent El Garces Hotel is undergoing long-term renovation into a historical museum.

From Needles, it's a quick 25-mile drive north along the Colorado River into Nevada to visit the gambling center of **Laughlin**. Since the mid-1980s Laughlin has boomed into a sparkling city with huge casinos and over 10,000 cheap rooms.

Needles was the boyhood home of Snoopy and Charlie Brown cartoonist **Charles Schulz** and is featured in the comic strips as the desert home of Snoopy's raffish sibling, Spike.

If you're set on traveling as much of the old road as possible, another stretch of Route 66 runs west of Needles and north of I-40 through the near-ghost towns of Goffs and Fenner, on a roller coaster of undulating two-lane blacktop, parallel to the railroad tracks.

Old Route 66 Loop: Ludlow and Amboy

Thanks to the orderly planners of the Santa Fe Railroad, which first blazed this route across the desert in 1883, many of the place names on this old Route 66 loop come in alphabetical order: from west to east, you have Amboy, Bristol, Cadiz,

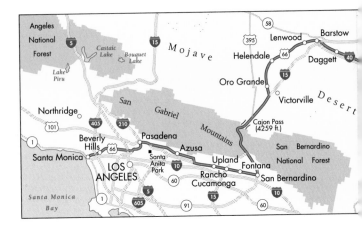

Danby, Essex, Fenner, Goffs, Home, Ibis, Java, and Klinefelter. Yes, Klinefelter.

If you want a quick and convincing taste of what traveling across the Mojave Desert was like in the days before air-conditioning and cellular phones, keep your eyes peeled for Historic Route 66 signs, and turn south off I-40 and follow the National Old Trails Highway, one of the many monikers Route 66 has carried over the years, on a 75-mile loop along the old road. Heading west, the loop leaves I-40 about 25 miles beyond Needles; heading east, the old road turns off I-40 at **Ludlow,** 50 miles east of Barstow, where two gas stations, a coffee shop, and a motel represent a major outpost of civilization.

While the drive alone is worth the extra time it takes, the real attraction comes midway along this old road loop: **Amboy** (pop. 2), which is synonymous with **Roy's Motel and Café,** a museum-worthy assembly of roadside architecture that has survived solely due to the willpower of its longtime lord and master, Buster Burris, who ran the place from 1938 (when he married the daughter of owner Roy Crowl) until 2000, when Buster died at the age of 92. In the late 1940s, Roy's was the prime stop between Needles and Barstow, and as many as 90 people staffed the café, the motel, and the car repair shop, working around the clock to cater to the thousands of passing

Huge chunks of the Mojave Desert have been used as military training grounds since World War II, when **General George Patton** used this area to prepare his tank battalions for battle in the North African desert. As many as 90,000 soldiers were based here during the war years; the remains of the camp can still be seen in the desert along Crucero Road, just north of the I-40 Ludlow exit.

junction with Hwy-64, which heads up (and up) to the east entrance of Grand Canyon National Park. A mile north of the Hwy-64 junction, along the south bank of the Little Colorado River, historic **Cameron Trading Post** (which also has a $120-a-night motel and an RV park; 520/679-2231) stands next to an equally historic one-lane suspension bridge, built in 1911 (and now carrying an oil pipeline). Cameron makes a good alternative to Tusayan, in case all the Grand Canyon's in-park accommodations are full.

From Cameron, Hwy-64 runs west along the Little Colorado River Gorge, which Hopi cosmology considers to be the place where man emerged into the present world. This deep canyon leads into the much larger Grand Canyon, while Hwy-64 climbs up the plateau for 30 miles to the east entrance of Grand Canyon National Park. Your first overlook is a desert view, where the photogenic 1930s Watchtower gives a great taste of the canyon from the highest point on the South Rim.

Williams

The last Route 66 town to be bypassed by I-40, **Williams** (pop. 2,842; elev. 6,780 ft) held out until the bitter end, waging court battle after court battle before finally surrendering on October 13, 1984. Despite the town's long opposition, in the end Williams gave in gracefully, going so far as to hold a

celebration-cum-wake for the old road, highlighted by a performance atop a new freeway overpass by none other than Mr. Route 66 himself, Bobby "Get Your Kicks" Troup.

Williams today is primarily a gateway to the Grand Canyon, but it also takes full tourist advantage of its Route 66 heritage: The downtown streets sport old-fashioned street lamps, and every other store sells a variety of Route 66 souvenirs, making the town much more than a pit stop for Grand Canyon–bound travelers. Apart from the Route 66 connections, Williams's pride and joy is the vintage **Grand Canyon Railway,** which whistles and steams its way north to the canyon every morning March–December, taking roughly two hours each way. Call for current schedules and fares (round-trip costs around $60; 800/843-8724), or stop by the historic depot, a former Harvey House hotel restored in 1990.

For an easy way to wake up, enjoy fresh pastries and a great

Grand Canyon National Park

One of the wonders of the natural world, the Grand Canyon of the Colorado River—two hundred miles long, a mile deep, and anywhere from five to 15 miles across—defies description, and if you're anywhere nearby you really owe it to yourself to stop for a look. The most amazing thing about the Grand Canyon, apart from its sheer size and incredible variety of shapes and colors, is how different it looks when viewed from different places (artist David Hockney has said that the Grand Canyon is the only place on Earth that makes you want to look in all directions—up, down, and side to side—at the same time), so be sure to check it out from as many angles, and at as many different times of day, as you can. A book like this one can do little more than hint at all there is to see and do, but if you have time for nothing else, take a quick hike down into the canyon to get a real sense of its truly awesome scale.

The great majority of the more than five million people who visit the Grand Canyon each year arrive at the South Rim and gaze down into the Grand Canyon from Mather Point, where the entrance road hits the edge of the gorge. The park visitors center and most of the food and lodging are located a mile west at Grand Canyon Village. Beyond Grand Canyon Village, West Rim Drive winds west, leading past the J. W. Powell Memorial at Hopi Point (from where you get great views of the Colorado River, which otherwise can be

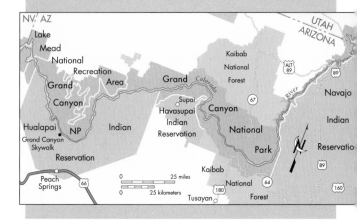

surprisingly hard to see) and a series of other viewpoints before ending up at Hermit's Rest, eight miles from Grand Canyon Village—where there are yet more stupendous views as well as restrooms, drinking fountains, and a gift shop.

The **West Rim Drive,** which was built for tourists by the Santa Fe Railroad in 1912, is closed to cars throughout summer, but frequent shuttle buses stop at all the viewpoints. A seven-mile hiking trail runs west from the Powell Memorial to Hermit's Rest, and a three-mile paved nature trail links the Powell Memorial with Grand Canyon Village.

East from Mather Point, **East Rim Drive** runs for 25 miles, stopping first at aptly named Grandview Point, 12 miles from Grand Canyon Village and a half mile north of the East Rim Drive. This is, literally and figuratively, a high point of any Grand Canyon tour, giving a 270-degree panorama over the entire gorge. Continuing east, the road passes a small prehistoric pueblo at Tusayan Ruins before ending with a bang at **Desert View Watchtower,** an Anasazi-style tower set right at the edge of the canyon. Though it looks ancient, the tower was created for tourists in 1932, designed by Mary Colter, also the architect of the Bright Angel Lodge and most of the wonderful old Harvey House hotels that lined Route 66 across the Southwest.

From the watchtower, the road continues along the rim through the east entrance, then drops down to the crossroads town of Cameron and the Little Colorado River.

Grand Canyon Hikes

To get a real feel for the Grand Canyon, you have to get out of the car, get beyond the often overcrowded viewpoints that line the South Rim, and take a walk down into the depths of the canyon itself. The most popular and best-maintained path, the **Bright Angel Trail,** descends from the west end of Grand Canyon Village, following a route blazed by prospectors in the 1890s. It's an all-day, 17-mile hike down to the Colorado River and back, but there are rest stops (with water) along the way. A shorter day hike cuts off to **Plateau Point,** 1,300 feet above the river and a

(continued on next page)

Grand Canyon National Park (continued)

12-mile round-trip from the South Rim. If you can finagle a reservation, you can extend the stay (and delay the climb back up) by staying overnight at Phantom Ranch, another three miles from Plateau Point on the north side of the Colorado River, which is traversed by a pair of suspension bridges. Nearby **Bright Angel Campground** has space for more than 100 people, but reservations and a backcountry camping permit are required; call the main visitors center for details.

Another interesting old trail drops down from Grandview Point to Horseshoe Mesa, where you can still see the remnants of an old copper mine that closed in 1907. This is a six-mile round-trip and gives an unforgettable introduction to the Grand Canyon.

No matter where you go, when hiking down into the canyon remember that it will take you twice as long to hike back up again, that the rim can be covered in snow and ice as late as June, and *always carry water*—especially in summer—at least a quart for every hour you're on the trail. The very good **visitors center** (520/638-7888) in Grand Canyon Village has information about the park's many hiking trails, the canyon's geology, the burro rides that take you down and back up again, and anything else to do with the Grand Canyon.

Practicalities

It may give a sense of the immensity of the Grand Canyon to know that, while the North Rim is a mere 6–10 miles from the South Rim as the crow flies, to get there by road requires a drive of at least 215 miles.

Most of what you'll need to know to enjoy your Grand Canyon visit is contained in the brochure you're given at the entrance, where you pay the $20-per-car fee (Golden Eagle and other passes are accepted).

To make advance reservations for accommodations—a good idea at any time of year but essential in the peak summer months—phone the park concessionaire, **Xanterra** (888/297-2757 in advance, 928/638-3283 same-day), which

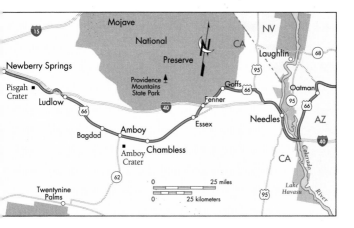

cars. Roy's fell on hard times after the opening of I-40 in 1974, but the whole town—complete with a huge "Roy's" sign, a classic late-1940s roadside café, a set of simple motor court cabins, and a pair of gas pumps—has hung on. Now, thanks to owner Albert Okura (who also owns the San Berdoo "First McDonald's" museum, described in this chapter), the café and gas station are open as often as possible, and Amboy is used as a film and photo-shoot location as well as being a photogenic reminder of the heyday of Route 66.

From Amboy, you can leave Route 66 and head south to the lovely high desert of Joshua Tree National Park, and the newly re-energized, 1950s "Rat Pack"–era resorts of Palm Springs. Staying on Route 66, you'll pass the lava flows around Amboy Crater, and you may see and hear helicopters and "Warthog" fighters playing war games on the huge Twentynine Palms Marine Corps base that stretches off to the south. At nearly 1,000 square miles, it's the largest base in the country and often the last US stop for personnel bound for battle in the Middle East.

More than 1.5 million acres between I-40 and I-15 have been set aside as the Mojave National Preserve. One of many

Detour: Las Vegas

Viva Las Vegas! Since its founding 100 years ago, Las Vegas has been the biggest, brightest, and brazenest boomtown in the history of the world. In the past 20 years, the population has more than tripled (rapidly approaching 2 million people in the metropolitan area), and over a dozen major hotels and megaresorts have re-created everything from ancient Egypt to Venice (complete with canals and gondoliers), Paris (a mock Eiffel Tower), and New York City (with a Coney Island roller coaster and fake steam puffing up from fake sidewalks). More numbers: With more than 150,000 rooms, the city has as many as New York and Chicago combined, and 40 million visitors lose close to $10 billion in the casinos here every year.

In addition to gambling, Las Vegas casinos have all the rooms, restaurants, and recreational opportunities you can imagine (and then some). If you're staying overnight, you'll enter the wacky and somewhat wicked world of Las Vegas lodging. Rooms aren't the dirt-cheap bargains they were a decade or more ago; rates vary depending on the time of year, time of the week, and sometimes even the time of day, but count on spending at least $100 for a decent hotel room, and close to five times that for something special. You should definitely make reservations as early as you can; on Friday nights, or during a big convention or boxing match, the whole town is often sold out. A final note: If you'll be schlepping a lot of luggage, Las Vegas hotel rooms are a very long way from parking spaces in the high-rise garages and huge lots, but on the upside, parking is free. Here are a few of the many places you can play:

Caesars Palace (3570 Las Vegas Boulevard South; 702/731-7110 or 800/634-6001): Long before there was a Mirage; a New York, New York; a Bellagio; or a Venetian, there was

Caesars Palace. Though ancient by Las Vegas standards (Caesars opened in 1966 as the first "themed" hotel in Las Vegas), this is still one of the classiest and most famous places in town.

Hard Rock Hotel/Casino (4555 Paradise Road; 702/693-5000 or 800/473-7625): For anyone under 60, this is the coolest place in town. Off the Strip and small by Vegas standards, but where else can you listen to nonstop classic rock 'n' roll while playing Jimi Hendrix slot machines (a line of "Purple Haze" pays $200) or drinking a cocktail at the swim-up bar?

Luxor (3900 Las Vegas Boulevard South; 702/262-4000 or 800/288-1000): The most distinctive casino, Luxor is housed inside a mammoth (29-million-cubic-foot) glass pyramid at the southern end of the Strip. Above the casino, stage sets of city streets hold high-tech attractions: motion simulators, 3-D and IMAX movies, and virtual reality arcade games.

The Mirage (3400 Las Vegas Boulevard South; 702/791-7111 or 800/627-6667): This casino has its own rainforest, a 50,000-gallon aquarium, and white tigers on display (this is the home of Siegfried and Roy). Next door, at Treasure Island, a theatrical (and free) pirate show is staged right on the Strip every 90 minutes or so all day long.

Wynn Las Vegas (3131 Las Vegas Boulevard South; 702/770-7100 or 888/320-WYNN): Brought to you by the creator of Mirage and Bellagio, on the site of the historic Desert Inn (where billionaire recluse Howard Hughes used to live), this ultra-fashionable 2,700-suite oasis is the last word in high-end indulgence, with an on-site Ferrari dealership and some of the best restaurants in the country.

places here worth the trip is **Mitchell Caverns** ($4; 760/928-2586) at the center of Providence Mountains State Recreation Area, 25 miles north of I-40 at the end of Essex Road. South from Amboy spreads Joshua Tree National Park.

Newberry Springs: Bagdad Cafe

Running alongside the I-40 freeway for about 50 miles east of Barstow, old Route 66 survives as a sort of frontage road, passing little more than an occasional lava flow (like Pisgah Crater, where there's a pair of I-40 rest areas).

About 20 miles east of Barstow is the place that for many people symbolizes the quirky personality of Route 66: **Newberry Springs,** where the popular Percy Adlon movie *Bagdad Cafe* was shot at the town's one and only café, now also known as the **Bagdad Cafe** (760/257-3101). Welcoming and appropriately weird, considering its connections with the oddly endearing movie (which features a cast of drifters, a fat German magician, and Jack Palance!), the real-life Bagdad Café is not so much a restaurant as it is a semi-catered film set, staying in business as a pit stop for fans of off-beat European cinema who happen to find themselves in the middle of the Mojave Desert. Be sure to read and sign the guest book, which features heartfelt comments from hundreds of people who've made the trek here from all over the world. (Scandinavians and other Teutonic types seems especially well represented.)

Northeast of Barstow, **Calico Ghost Town** is an enjoyable resurrection of the silver mining camp that boomed here during the 1890s.

Between the Bagdad Café and Barstow, old Route 66 runs past the region's other unique claim to fame: the semi-successful **Solar One** and **Solar Two** power plants, experimental, 10-megawatt electricity generating stations north of I-40 that are now used as astronomical gamma-wave observatory.

Barstow

The burly railroad and transportation center of **Barstow** (pop. 21,495) is located in the middle of the Mojave Desert, at the point where I-40 disappears into I-15, midway between Los Angeles and Las Vegas. Trucks and trains are the main business in town—even the McDonald's pays homage to trains, with its dining rooms housed in old boxcars—and Barstow is scruffy and a little scary in the way railroad towns can be. Along Main Street, the old Route 66 corridor, many of the old cafés and motels are now closed and boarded up, but just north of old Route 66, the circa-1913 Harvey House **Casa del Desierto** hotel next to the train station is a survivor from an earlier age. Looking like the Doge's Palace in Venice (if the Doge's Palace faced the wide-open desert instead of an intricate network of canals . . .), the gothic-style arcades are a substantial reminder of a time when travel meant more than just getting somewhere. The long-abandoned building has been brought back to use as a railroad and Route 66 **museum** (Fri.–Sun. 11 AM–4 PM; 760/255-1890).

The **Mojave Desert** is one of the driest places on the planet; parts of it receive less than three inches of rainfall in an average year, sometimes going for more than two years without getting a drop.

Victorville

Between Barstow and Victorville, old Route 66 survives as an "old roads" trek across the Mojave Desert. The 36-mile route, called the National Old Trails Highway, parallels the railroad tracks and the usually parched Mojave River, passing through odd little towns like **Oro Grande,** which is still home to a huge cement plant and lots of roadside junk shops. Outside Barstow at the west end of Main Street, keep an eye out for the Christian Motorcycle club sign welcoming you to **Lenwood,** a crossroads near where the old road reconnects with I-15. The best reason to take the "old road" is that you'll be sure to enter Victorville on old Route 66 and see Victorville at its best: at the **California Route 66 Museum,** right on old Route 66, in Old Town across from the train station at 16825 D Street (Thurs.–Mon.; 760/951-0436), where a small but growing collection of road signs, photographs, and reminiscences helps preserve the life and times of the great old highway. The museum also holds most of the surviving pieces of Hula Ville, an outdoor sculpture park and oddball art gallery that used to stand west of Victorville; most of the paintings and hand-lettered memorials to sundry bums, hobos, and other travelers he called his friends were moved here after Hula Ville's 100-year-old creator and caretaker, the former carnival worker "Fry Pan" Miles Mahan, passed away in 1996.

Without the Route 66 connections,

however, Victorville would be just another distant SoCal commuter suburb; in fact, ever since the departure of Hula Ville, not to mention the wonderful Roy Rogers and Dale Evans Museum, which—along with its much-loved celebrity subjects—had a home here, Victorville just hasn't seemed the same. Fortunately old Route 66 can still be traced through town: from the Route 66 Museum, turn south onto 7th Street, which runs past a few neon-signed old motels like the **New Corral** ($50; 760/245-9378) at 14643 7th Street with its animated bucking bronco, and the large **Best Western Green Tree Inn** ($80; 760/245-3461), just off the freeway at 14173 Green Tree Boulevard.

South and west of Victorville, heading toward Los Angeles and the seemingly distant Pacific Ocean, a number of very picturesque but generally dead-end stretches of old Route 66 go over **Cajon Pass,** but the main road is definitely I-15. At the top of the pass, turn off the freeway at the Oak Hills exit and stop for a burger and fries at the **Summit Inn** (760/949-1313 or 760/949-8688), one of the few survivors of the old road businesses along this stretch of highway.

San Bernardino

Sometimes known as "San Berdoo," in the 1940s and 1950s the city of **San Bernardino** (pop. 190,000) was where Maurice and Richard McDonald perfected the burger–making restaurant chain that bears their name. In 1961, the McDonald brothers sold their company to Ray Kroc, and the rest is fast-food history. Though the original buildings were demolished decades ago, the location is now home to an

unofficial, ad hoc museum, displaying McDonalds and Route 66 memorabilia at 1398 N. "E" Street (free; 909/885-6324).

From downtown San Bernardino, which somewhat confusingly is actually a dozen miles east of the I-15 freeway, the old Route 66 alignment headed west along Foothill Boulevard, where a remnant of old Route 66 road culture still survives: the 19 concrete tepees that form the **Wigwam Motel,** at 2728 W. Foothill Boulevard (around $70; 909/875-3005).

San Bernardino County, which covers over 20,000 square miles (most of it desert), is the largest in the United States.

Once as seedy as its "Do It In A TeePee" sign suggested, this Wigwam (one of three in the world—another sits along Route 66 in Holbrook, Arizona) has been fully updated and once again welcomes travelers interested in offbeat accommodations (with a swimming pool and barbecues in between the tepees).

San Bernardino is home to the Class A farm club of the L.A. Dodgers, and the team name plays up the Route 66 connections: they're called the **Inland Empire 66ers.** The stadium is right off the old road at 280 S. "E" Street ($6 and up; 909/888-9922). Games are broadcast on **KCAA 1050 AM.**

From the Wigwam Motel, Foothill Boulevard runs west through the post-industrial city of Fontana, birthplace of the Hell's Angels' Motorcycle Club (and L.A. culture critic Mike Davis), before passing by another great old road landmark: **Bono's Giant Orange,** an orange-shaped stand that, during the 1920s, offered thirsty Route 66 travelers "All The Orange Juice You Can Drink—10¢." The original orange grove is now a Wal-Mart, and the Giant Orange was moved next to a now-closed café (at 15395 Foothill Boulevard) where it's in good shape—and slated for eventual reopening as a juice stand. Bono's Giant Orange is one of the last of the dozens of giant orange-shaped roadside businesses all over California, which used to tempt passersby to stop and sample their wares. Others survive in the Central Valley (near Chowchilla along Hwy-99, and in Dixon off I-80), but this is the best preserved of them all.

San Gabriel Valley

Winding between Pasadena and San Bernardino, along the foothills of the sometimes-snowcapped San Gabriel Mountains, old Route 66 links a number of once-distinct communities like **Azusa,** home of the classic Foothill Drive-In, whose marquee was saved when the land was recently developed, and collegiate **Claremont.** In **Upland,** where the old road features a number of recently installed retro–Route 66 streetlamps, there's a grass

median strip graced by a statue of the pioneer Madonna of the Trail, which officially marked the western end of the National Old Trails Highway, the immediate precursor to Route 66.

The San Gabriel Valley takes its name from old **Mission San Gabriel Arcangel,** which still stands at 537 W. Mission Drive (daily 9 AM–4 PM; $1; 626/457-3035). Despite suffering extensive earthquake damage, the mission is an interesting spot, though not as evocative as others in the chain.

Rancho Cucamonga (pop. 125,000), is now best known as the home of the Epicenter, where the very popular Angels farm club, the **Cucamonga Quakes** (909/481-5000), play Class A baseball, and a statue of Jack Benny welcomes you through the turnstiles. (If you ever heard Benny's long-running radio and TV show, which featured Mel Blanc reading the tag line "Anaheim, Azusa, and CU-CA-MON-GA," you'll know why he's there.)

The town of **Monrovia** holds another Route 66 survivor: the groovy, Mesoamerican-style art deco exuberance of the **Aztec Hotel,** at 311 W. Foothill Boulevard (626/358-3231), better for the bar (which hosts frequent live music) than for its unrestored rooms, but well worth a look. Monrovia was home for many years to quixotic author Upton Sinclair (1878–1968) and is now the headquarters of the cult-favorite grocery store Trader Joe's, which started in Pasadena in 1958.

In the next town to the west, **Sierra Madre,** Foothill Boulevard runs past the landmark racetrack at **Santa Anita,** designed by Hoover Dam stylist Gordon Kaufmann. The Marx Brothers filmed *A Day at the Races* here, but the art deco facades are threatened by the track's ongoing "improvement" into a Las Vegas–style Wild West theme park.

Huntington Museum and Gardens

East of Pasadena, at the west end of the San Gabriel Valley, old Route 66 runs along Huntington Drive, which takes its name from one of the most important figures in early Los Angeles, Henry Huntington. Nephew of Southern Pacific Railroad baron Collis P. Huntington, from whom Henry inherited a huge fortune (as well as a wife, Arabella), Henry Huntington controlled most of southern California's once-extensive public transit system. He is now most remembered for creating and endowing one of the world's great museums, the **Huntington Library, Museum and Gardens,** located in the exclusive community of San Marino at 1151 Oxford Road (closed Mon.; 626/405-2141).

The Huntington Library contains all sorts of unique books and documents and preserves thousands more for the benefit of scholars, but the real draw is the art gallery, which displays an excellent collection of British and European painting and sculpture, with major works by Reynolds, Gainsborough, and others. There are also fine assemblages of American art, including Gilbert Stuart's familiar portrait of George Washington. Perhaps the best part of the Huntington is its splendid **gardens,** which cover 120 acres in a series of mini-ecosystems, distilling the essence of Australia, Japan, South America, and, in the country's largest cactus garden, the American Southwest.

Pasadena

Heading out of downtown Los Angeles, the historic Pasadena Freeway (Hwy-110) drops you off unceremoniously short of **Pasadena,** but following Figueroa Street brings you in with a bang on the soaring **Colorado Boulevard Bridge,** an elegant-ly arching, circa-1913 concrete bridge at the western edge of Pasadena, which long marked the symbolic entrance to Los Angeles from the east.

Colorado Boulevard in Pasadena holds the annual **Tournament of Roses Parade,** every New Year's Day before the famous Rose Bowl football game.

Recently restored, the bridge spans **Arroyo Seco** along the south side of the Ventura Freeway (Hwy-134). Arroyo Seco itself is full of significant sights, including college football's Rose Bowl and some of the most important architecture in Southern California, notably the **Gamble House,** a 100-year-old arts-and-crafts gem at 4 Westmoreland Place (Thurs.–Sun. afternoons; $10; 626/793-3334). Above the arroyo, on old Route 66 at 411 W. Colorado Boulevard, the **Norton Simon Museum** (closed Tues.; $8; 626/449-6840) has a medium-sized but impeccably chosen collection of western and southeast Asian art, ranging from Hindu sculpture to one the world's foremost collections of Degas paintings, drawings, and sculptures.

Just a few blocks east of Arroyo Seco and the Norton Simon Museum down old Route 66, Old Pasadena is the new name for the old center of town, where locals congregate for evening fun and daytime shopping. Start your morning with breakfast at **Marston's** (626/796-2459), just north of Old Pasadena at 151 E. Walnut Street, or detour two blocks south of old Route 66 to enjoy the fine neon sign and classic soda-fountain milk shakes at the **Fair Oaks Pharmacy,** 1526 Mission Street (626/799-1414). There are quite a few old motels along this stretch of Route 66; one good bet is the **Saga Motor Hotel,** 1633 E. Colorado Boulevard ($99 and up; 626/795-0431).

Route 66 Across Los Angeles

Diehard old-road fans will be pleasantly surprised to know that Route 66 across Los Angeles still exists, almost completely intact. West from Pasadena into downtown L.A., you have your choice of Route 66 routings. You can hop onto the Pasadena Freeway (Hwy-110) for a trip back to freeways past: Opened in 1939, when it was called the Arroyo Seco Parkway, this was California's first freeway and featured such novel (and never repeated) concepts as 15-mph exit ramps and stop signs at the entrances. Or, you can follow Figueroa, which in L.A. lingo is known as a "surface street," running parallel to the freeway past some fascinating pieces of Los Angeles new and old, including the concrete-lined Los Angeles River, hilltop Dodger Stadium, and the excellent **Gene Autry Museum of the American West** at Griffth's Park (closed Mon.; $9; 323/667-2000), a phenomenally wide-ranging collection featuring Native American art and artifacts from all over western North America, as well as "Wild West" ephemera and pop culture icons. (The museum was established by Hollywood's "Singing Cowboy," Gene Autry, a media magnate who is the only person ever awarded five stars on the Hollywood Walk of Fame.)

Though it's now effectively swallowed up in Southern California's never-ending sprawl, the **San Gabriel Valley** used to be the westbound traveler's first taste of Southern California. After crossing the Mojave Desert and the high mountains, Route 66 dropped down into what might have seemed like paradise: Orange groves as far as the eye could see, a few tidy towns linked by streetcars, and houses draped in climbing roses and bougainvillea.

Besides all the sights, Route 66 across L.A. also holds two of the city's best bookshops: **Book Soup,** in West Hollywood at 8818 Sunset Strip, and **Vroman's,** in Pasadena at 695 E. Colorado Blvd.

Now marked by prominent beige road signs reading "Historic Route 66 1935–1964," old Route 66 follows Sunset Boulevard from the historic core of the city, starting at Olvera Street and the Plaza de Los Angeles State Historic Park, before winding west to Hollywood. In Hollywood itself, Route 66 turns onto Santa Monica Boulevard, then runs past the cemetery-cum-theme park **Hollywood Forever** (daily; free;

323/469-1181), where such luminaries as Rudolf Valentino and Mel Blanc are entombed, overlooked by the water tower of legendary Paramount Studios. It's a unique experience by day, and even more so on nights when the cemetery is host to "Midnight Movies," outdoor screenings of its residents' works.

Continuing west to the Pacific, old Route 66 follows Santa Monica Boulevard through the heart of West Hollywood and Beverly Hills, where "Mr. Route 66" himself, the Oklahoma-born comedian Will Rogers, once was mayor.

Santa Monica

Old Route 66 had its western terminus at the edge of the Pacific Ocean in **Santa Monica,** on a palm-lined bluff a few blocks north of the city's landmark pier. The pier holds a small amusement park and a lovely old Looff carousel (as seen in the movie *The Sting*). A beachfront walkway heads south of the pier to Venice Beach, heart of bohemian L.A., but near where Santa Monica Boulevard dead-ends at Ocean Boulevard, a brass plaque marks the official end of Route 66, the "Main Street of America," also remembered as the Will Rogers Highway, one of many names the old road earned in its half century of existence. The plaque remembers Rogers as a "Humorist, World Traveler, Good Neighbor"—not bad for an Okie from the middle of nowhere.

Two blocks east of the ocean, stretch your legs at Santa Monica Place and the adjacent Third Street Promenade, an indoor/outdoor shopping area and icon of contemporary Southern California (sub)urban culture. The surrounding streets are among the liveliest in Southern California; people actually walk, enjoying street performers, trendy cafés, bookshops, and movie theaters.

Enjoyable in its own right, Santa Monica also makes a very good base for seeing the rest of the L.A. area. For the full retro-luxury experience, check in to the art deco **Georgian Hotel,** at 1415 Ocean Avenue ($250 and up; 310/395-9945). Or you can save your money for food and fun by staying at the very popular **HI-Santa Monica Hostel** (around $25 per person; 310/393-9913) at 1436 2nd Street.

Los Angeles

Love it or hate it, one thing you can't do about L.A. is ignore it. Thanks to Hollywood in all its many guises (movies, television, the music industry), the city is always in the headlines. Without falling too deeply under the spell of its hyperbole-fueled image-making machinery, it's safe to say that

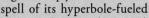
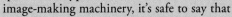

L.A. definitely has something for everyone. In keeping with its car-centered culture, however, our suggested tour ignores the many individual attractions and focuses instead on a pair of quintessential L.A. drives.

Winding along the crest of the Hollywood Hills, **Mulholland Drive** is the classic L.A. cruise. Starting in the east within sight of the Hollywood Sign and the Hollywood Bowl, this ribbon of two-lane blacktop passes by the city's most valuable real estate, giving great views on both sides, both by day and after dark.

Another classic L.A. cruise, running from the scruffy fringes of downtown all the way west to the coast, **Sunset Boulevard** gives glimpses into almost every conceivable aspect of Los Angeles life. Starting downtown, the historic core of colonial Los Angeles and now a showcase of contemporary architecture thanks to a stunning new cathedral and concert hall, Sunset Boulevard's 27-mile course then winds west past Echo Park and Hollywood to West Hollywood, where it becomes the Sunset Strip, still the liveliest nightclub district in town. Continuing west, Sunset winds through Beverly Hills, Brentwood, and Bel-Air, lined by the largest mansions you're likely to see, before ending up at the edge of the Pacific Ocean.

Practicalities

Most flights into Los Angeles arrive at Los Angeles International Airport (LAX), on the coast southwest of downtown, where you'll find all the usual shuttles and rent-al car agencies. Other useful L.A. airports include Bob Hope (BUR) in Burbank, and John Wayne (SNA), in Orange County.

Before choosing a place to stay, think about where you want to spend your time and settle near there. High-end places abound, but character can be hard to come by. Along the coast, recommended accommodations range from the handy **Santa Monica HI Hostel** ($25 per person; 310/393-9913), a block from the beach at 1436 2nd Street, to the unique **Hotel Queen Mary** in Long Beach ($109 and up; 562/435-3511), offering authentic art deco–era staterooms in the fabulous old luxury liner. Mid-range with a great mid-city location, try the **Farmer's Daughter** ($149 and up; 800/334-1658), next to the historic Farmer's Market at 115 S. Fairfax Avenue, a very friendly 1950s-style motel with tons of charm and the city's hottest new shopping mall and entertainment complex, The Grove, across the street. Downtown, the most fabulous place to stay is the retro-1960s **Downtown Standard,** 550 S. Flower Street ($175 and up; 213/892-8080), with the world's coolest rooftop, poolside bar.

For food, one place I always try to stop is the **Apple Pan** (310/475-3585), at 10801 W. Pico Boulevard, an ancient (circa-1947) landmark on the West L.A. landscape, serving the best hamburgers on the planet—though I'll admit to being biased, since I grew up eating them. Take a seat at the counter, and be sure to save room for a slice of the wonderful fruit pies. Late at night, the huge sandwiches and heart-warming soups at **Canter's Deli,** 419 N. Fairfax Avenue (open daily 24 hours; 213/651-2030), draws all kinds of night owls to a lively New York–style deli in the heart of the predominantly Jewish Fairfax District. Downtown, in the heart of old L.A. at 1001 Alameda, **Philippe's French Dip Sandwiches** (213/628-3781) is a classic working man's cafeteria, offering good food at impossibly low prices, with character to spare.

The **Los Angeles Dodgers** (323/224-1471) play at beautiful Dodger Stadium, on a hill above downtown.

The usual array of information about hotels, restaurants, tickets to TV show tapings, and all other L.A.-area attractions is available through the **Los Angeles Convention and Visitors Bureau** (213/689-8822 or 800/228-2452), with an office at 685 S. Figueroa Street.

108

Index

Photo and Illustration Credits

Avalon Travel logo is the property of Avalon Travel, a member of the Perseus Books Group. All other marks and logos depicted are the property of the original owners. All rights reserved.

All vintage postcards, photographs, and maps in this book from the private collection of Jamie Jensen, unless otherwise credited.

Photos © Jamie Jensen: pages 13, 19, 28, 34, 36, 37, 47, 49, 51 photo © Jamie Jensen, Cadillac Ranch © Ant Farm; 53, 54, 55, 66, 72, 86, 95

United States Quarter-Dollar Coin Images
State quarter-dollar coin images from the United States Mint. Used with permission.

United States Postage Stamps
All postage stamps © United States Postal Service. All rights reserved. Used with permission. Written authorization from the Postal Service is required to use, reproduce, post, transmit, distribute, or publicly display these images.

Pages 8, 19, 31, 33, 48, 53, 68, 93 Greetings from America Series Stamp Designs © 2002 United States Postal Service; 83 Grand Canyon National Park © 1998 United States Postal Service.

Additional credits:
Page 11 Grant Wood, American Gothic, 1930. The Art Institute of Chicago: Friends of American Art Collection; 12 © Valerie Zona-Baxter / flickr.com; 14, 40 © Shellee Graham; 15 © Illinois State Tourism; 17, 88 © Bob Waldmire; 24 © Steve Wallace / Flickr.com; 57 © Frank Schmidt; 62 © Brian Bennett / Flickr.com; 75 © Lazy SOB Records; 77 Courtesy of Flagstaff Convention & Visitors Bureau; 85 Courtesy of Arizona Department of Tourism/Photograph by Hoshino; 92 © Out West Newspaper; 96, 97 © Las Vegas News Bureau; 105 © Doug Pappas

Cover Images:
Cover postcards from the private collections of Domini Dragoone, Jamie Jensen, and Kevin Roe. For original publisher information, see *Road Trip USA*, 5th edition (Avalon Travel, 2009).